PROTOCOL PACKAGES

The Instructional Design Library

Volume 31

PROTOCOL PACKAGES

Sivasailam Thiagarajan
Instructional Alternatives
Bloomington, Indiana

Danny G. Langdon
Series Editor

Educational Technology Publications
Englewood Cliffs, New Jersey 07632

Library of Congress Cataloging in Publication Data

Thiagarajan, Sivasailam.
    Protocol packages.

        (The Instructional design library; v. 31)
        Bibliography: p.
        1. Interaction analysis in education. 2. Inter-
personal relations. I. Title. II. Series: Instructional design library; v. 31.
LB1033.T48   371.1'02   79-23503
ISBN 0-87778-151-6

Copyright © 1980 Educational Technology Publications, Inc., Englewood Cliffs, New Jersey 07632.

Printed in the United States of America.

Library of Congress Catalog Card Number:
79-23503.

International Standard Book Number:
0-87778-151-6.

First Printing: March, 1980.

FOREWORD

The "real world" has long been viewed as an ideal environment in which to learn. Just how the real world is to be taken advantage of from a learning standpoint—other than experiencing, as people are often heard to say, "the school of hard knocks," or in an experiential manner of let's see what happens—has not been readily determined. Perhaps it is the uncontrolled nature of the real world which makes it difficult to use, and rightly so. Thus, we fall back on designs, such as simulations and role playing, to meet our needs and experiences in approximations as close to the real world as these designs are capable of providing. An instructional design which allows us at least to visualize and "audiotize" the real world just as it is—or capture it as closely on film, video, and tape—and then do something with it on a meaningful level is the protocol package.

As the author is careful to note, protocol packages are not capable of capturing completely (and realistically) the real world, nor can they be used to teach anything and everything from the real world. They can be used effectively, however, with one major aspect of our real-world environment which is a major concern of education and training. This is the world of human interactions. The author points to six particular aspects of instruction for which the protocol package is especially suitable: increasing awareness levels, providing advance organizers, modeling of skills, providing a stimulus for discussion, teaching concepts, and training for an observation system. The reader will particularly appreciate the attention given to the use and development of protocol packages for the teaching of concepts.

This is an exceptionally fine instructional design. Those in training will find in it many practical applications; those in education will find it a convenient design for bringing a close approximation of the real world into the classroom.

Danny G. Langdon
Series Editor

PREFACE

Most of the major research and development activities on protocol materials have been in the area of teacher education, where the Bureau of Educational Personnel Development (BEPD) of the U.S. Office of Education provided substantial financial support in the late 1960's. My exposure to this instructional format began during this affluent period when I worked as a research associate for Dr. David Gliessman, one of the leaders of the protocol movement. Although I moved on to other areas of instructional development within a year, I kept up my interest in protocol materials.

I believe that this movement failed to live up to its promises in spite of the best intents of its leaders. This is perhaps due to the fact that the university professors who were funded to direct various projects neglected the diffusion issues, concentrated on form to the detriment of the substance, ignored established processes of systematic instructional development, and preferred scholarly categorization to practical utility.

My interest in protocol materials was revived during the time I worked at Indiana University's Center for Innovation in Teaching the Handicapped. During the early 1970's, I was engaged in producing training materials for observers using standardized interaction systems for recording teacher-pupil behaviors in the classrooms. Most of the examples used in this book are based on the work I did with Dr. William W. Lynch, Dr. Albert H. Fink, and Dr. Melvyn I. Semmel. I have distorted some of their conceptual categories in order to illustrate various instructional points. The credit for the original conceptualization belongs to these scholars, and the responsibility for all inaccuracies and inconsistencies is mine.

During the last few years, I have become increasingly aware of the application of protocol packages to areas other than teacher training. I realized their potential role in second-language and cross-cultural training through my activities and arguments with Dr. Harold Stolovitch of the University of Montreal. And my recent work as a free-lance training consultant to business and industry suggested the broader application of protocol materials to different types of training, which involves interaction among people.

This book is a presentation of the world of protocols according to a somewhat subjective view of mine. As I re-read the chapters, I am aware of the great extent to which this view has been influenced by the work of one person in the area of instructional design in general and concept analysis in particular. With grateful thanks for her inputs and encouragement, I dedicate this book to Dr. Susan M. Markle.

S.T.

CONTENTS

FOREWORD v

PREFACE vii

ABSTRACT xi

I. USE 3

II. OPERATIONAL DESCRIPTION 25

III. DESIGN FORMAT 43

IV. OUTCOMES 81

V. DEVELOPMENTAL GUIDE 89

VI. RESOURCES 113

ABSTRACT

PROTOCOL PACKAGES

A protocol is an authentic, replayable record of interactive human behavior. A protocol package is an instructional design that incorporates a protocol and helps trainees acquire basic concepts and analytical skills related to a specific, interpersonal domain.

A protocol package contains two components: The first (called the protocol component) presents examples of interactive behaviors. This component can be analyzed into the design elements of the conceptual domain, superordinate concepts, individual concepts, and critical attributes. The scope and sequence of the examples are determined by a systematic concept analysis. Usually this component includes a wide range of divergent examples and a number of subtle nonexamples arranged in a sequence that facilitates attending to the critical and variable attributes of individual concepts and to the interrelationships among them. The second component (called the instructional component) contains instructional messages and activities. These include labels for the concepts, lists of their critical and variable attributes, definitions, practical exercises, cues, commentaries, and feedback to the trainee.

A salient outcome of the protocol package is the acquisition of a conceptual base for the analysis of interpersonal situations. An important outcome which is missing in the protocol package is practical skill training. While protocol packages are effective tools for presenting a theoretical base, they have to be supplemented by skill training that involves active participation in a real or simulated interaction.

Systematic development of a protocol package involves the stages of analysis, design, production, evaluation/revision, and implementation. Design considerations involve a choice among different media, production techniques (e.g., scripted versus natural events), and different degrees of editing. Both expert evaluation and learner verification provide useful feedback to improve the instructional effectiveness of the protocol package.

PROTOCOL PACKAGES

I.

USE

One meaning of the word *protocol*, according to my *Random House Dictionary of the English Language*, is "a report of an observation exactly and without attempting an interpretation." Social scientists have long used protocols—descriptive records written during (or immediately after) their observations—to provide a pool of information for leisurely analysis at a later time. Thus, for example, ethnologists recorded religious ceremonies of a remote tribe, ethologists recorded the behavior of gorillas in their natural habitat, developmental psychologists recorded the responses of an infant to novel stimuli, and social psychologists recorded the activities of a mob during a political rally. Later, these scientists sifted through their protocols, analyzed and reanalyzed the data, and identified consistent patterns and cause-effect relationships.

With the advent of electronic recording devices, a new approach to protocols has become popular. Scientists are now able to capture raw behaviors on audiotape and/or videotape in a more unbiased form than written protocols. With these replayable recordings, they are able to repeatedly analyze the original events. An unobtrusive video camera in a classroom or an automated audio system in a therapist's office captures valuable data about human interactions and their consequences.

3

Interest in the use of protocols as an educational tool began with the work of Smith and his colleagues (1969) in the area of teacher training. In the book *Teachers for the Real World,* the Smith Committee complains that

> ... teachers fail because they have not been trained calmly to analyze new situations against a firm background of relevant theory. Typically, they base their interpretations of behavior on intuition and common sense ... If the teacher is incapable of understanding classroom situations, the actions he (sic) takes will often increase his (sic) difficulties. (pp. 28-29)

As a solution to this problem, the committee recommends the systematic training of teachers to objectively analyze classroom interactions using concepts and principles from different disciplines. It also suggests that the analytical approach of a social scientist can be adapted for instructional purposes by using protocol materials from real classrooms as tools for teacher preparation. By systematically producing protocol materials of student interaction in classrooms, playgrounds, and other places, it is possible to provide a glimpse of the real teaching world to preservice teachers. By attempting to interpret the educationally significant events in these protocol recordings, teachers in training gain skills for applying appropriate concepts from such fields as psychology, sociology, anthropology, and philosophy.

A Working Definition of Protocols

The rest of this chapter explains different uses of protocols and provides an example to illustrate each use. In order to benefit from these explanations and examples, we need a common definition of *protocol.* The next chapter provides a detailed definition; for our current needs, let us use this definition which has come to be accepted in teacher training circles: *A protocol is an authentic, replayable record of interactive behavior in its uninterpreted form.* Let us also define the more specific concept of *protocol packages* as *an instructional design format which incorporates a protocol and which is designed to help the trainee acquire a framework of interactive behavioral concepts.*

Figure 1 summarizes the different uses of protocol packages and also shows the organization of the rest of this chapter. What follows is a discussion of the use of protocols for instruction, evaluation of instruction, and analysis of instruction. Each specific use is illustrated by an example. Although the examples are fictional, they have all been drawn from real case studies.

Protocol Packages for Instruction

The major concern of this book is with the use of protocol packages for instructional purposes. Four of these instructional uses provide background information, while the last two deal directly with the acquisition of conceptual frameworks.

1. *Increasing awareness levels.* Protocol packages can be effectively used to increase trainees' familiarity with an area of human interaction which they are about to study in greater detail. Here is an example of this type of application:

Example 1. Where Did All the Snake Charmers Go?

The target population for this protocol package is volunteer workers who are about to be assigned to Peace Corps-like activities in various villages of South India. The objective for this protocol is to provide a background context of life in these villages. The package consists of a 30-minute videotape with an edited compilation of everyday activities from a typical South Indian village. It is played repeatedly during every evening of a two-week workshop at the trainees' lounge. No formal instruction is associated with the videotape. It becomes the background to the trainees' leisure time activities.

Figure 1

*Summary Chart of Different Uses
of Protocol Packages*

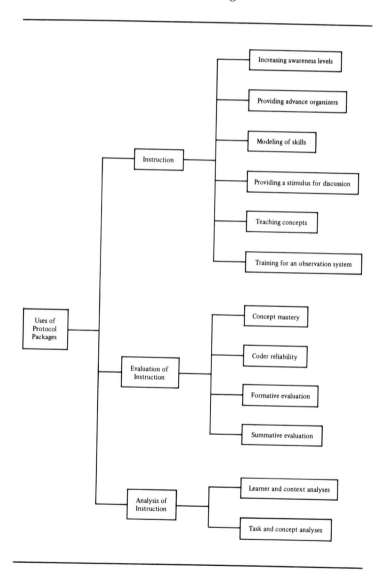

The segment does not have a host to provide any voice-over commentary interpreting or explaining what is happening. However, the material does include sounds recorded on location of people talking to each other in some unintelligible, local language. The music on the tape is the actual music being played during the local activity. The different scenes in the protocol merge with each other and appear to depict such situations as the following:

- *A busy day at the marketplace.*
- *A festival at the local temple.*
- *A crowded railroad station during the arrival and departure of a train.*
- *Outside the local movie theater after a show.*
- *The bed of a dried-up river with a group of children playing.*
- *A "classroom" in an open-air elementary school.*
- *A funeral procession.*
- *A marriage ceremony.*
- *The local pond with a group of women doing their laundry.*

The application of protocol packages does not result in the acquisition of any specific skills nor even specific concepts. However, it increases trainees' familiarity with some unknown piece of reality. Such "orientation" protocols may be used in other situations to reduce the "culture shock" that is brought on by a new environment.

2. *Providing advance organizers.* A related use of protocol packages is to provide a preview of a complex framework prior to detailed study of individual concepts. Here is an example of this type of application:

Example 2. Call the Ambulance and Keep Talking to Her

The target population for this protocol package is people who respond to callers on a drug abuse hotline telephone number which operates around the clock. The trainees come from all walks of life and have very little background in drugs or in counseling. The objective of this protocol package is to give an overview of various concepts used to analyze different types of telephone calls. The actual protocol is an audiotape recording of various authentic (but staged) telephone calls based on actual case histories. Trainees listen to these protocols with headphones. The voices sound as though they are coming over the telephone.

Each segment of this protocol is a short excerpt illustrating a specific type of telephone call. Each category is identified in the beginning by a narrator using such labels as "Level of Emergency: Urgent." Some of the excerpts are played more than once as examples of other classifications. The category system includes the following:

1. Level of emergency: leisurely, normal, urgent, . . .
2. Type of caller: self, friend, family, . . .
3. Inferred intent: information gathering, attention getting, treatment seeking, . . .
4. Caller's approach: friendly, hostile, defensive, . . .
5. Type of drug: . . .

Later in this training course, each of these categories is defined and its critical characteristics identified. After the trainees have acquired this conceptual base, they are taught a number of counseling techniques associated with each type of telephone call.

3. *Modeling of skills.* Protocol packages are associated with concepts, and training materials are associated with skills. While this is a convenient categorization for gross analysis, many skills incorporate concepts and vice versa. One area where concepts and skills merge with each other is in human interactions where no clear-cut, algorithmic procedures exist to direct the trainee on what to do and when to do it. In a situation like this, an effective training technique is to have the trainee observe a skilled performer and then model his or her performance. Here is an example of this kind of application of protocol packages:

Example 3. Clearing the Air

The target population for this protocol package is human relations trainers who will use a number of small-group activities in their training workshops. This protocol package is used as a part of a larger training module on how to conduct different types of small-group activities. More specifically, it is a part of the final module on how to conduct a debriefing session. The protocol shows experienced group leaders conducting the initial phase of debriefing during which they attempt to facilitate a catharsis of participants' feelings and emotions from an earlier experience. (After they get these feelings off their chests, they undertake systematic analysis of their experiences.)

The actual protocol presents seven different leaders debriefing their groups without any superimposed narration to explain what they are doing. The segments show groups of different sizes and different age levels. Each segment presents a debriefing session following a different type of small-group experience (e.g., simulation, field trip, psychodrama, open-ended role play, Role-map). The segments portray unrehearsed performances

---

from different debriefing sessions. Skillful and unobtrusive editing of the videotape ensures a comprehensive coverage of these component concepts in debriefing:
- *Initiating sharing of emotions.*
- *Prompting direct and authentic statements.*
- *Listening with respect.*
- *Handling emotional "outbursts."*
- *Concluding the session.*

The instructional design strategy of behavior modeling is very closely related to our concept of protocol packages. Debriefing is just one of the many interpersonal skills where direct instruction on what to do and what not to do is effectively supplemented by realistic instances of exemplary performance.

4. *Providing a stimulus for discussion.* Protocol packages are frequently designed to illustrate a predetermined conceptual framework for the analysis of human interaction. Sometimes, a protocol may portray an event (usually a critical one) to trigger off a discussion during which the trainees share their own conceptual frameworks with each other. Here is an example of this type of an open-ended application of a protocol:

Example 4. Shoplifting
The target population for this protocol film is fourth and fifth graders. The objective is to encourage a discussion of various ethical concepts involved in shoplifting. The material is a dramatic film which shows Mike suddenly finding out that some of his friends are regularly stealing things from local shops. He is worried and talks to his brother, only to find out that everybody does it. Mike's friends pressure him to join a gang to

carry out systematic shoplifting activities. Mike refuses to do so in spite of his friends' taunting. The toyshop sells a model airplane which Mike wants badly but does not have the money to buy. His father refuses to advance money from his weekly allowance. Mike is alarmed because the stock in the shop is getting low. He finally decides to steal the last model but bungles the job. He is caught by the shopkeeper, who, as the segment ends, is dialing the telephone.

The film is shown without any intruding narration. After the film, learners are divided into small groups to analyze what has happened in the film. They are supplied with a series of open-ended stimulus questions.

This protocol package contains a carefully structured group discussion to facilitate a joint analysis of the event. The instructional design format of Grouprograms (Thiagarajan, 1978) may be combined with protocol materials in this type of application.

5. *Teaching concepts.* Helping trainees to acquire a set of concepts so that they can use them to analyze real-life interactions is the major use of protocol packages. Here is an example of this application:

Example 5. My Perfect Right

The target population for this protocol package is adult learners in different occupations. This protocol is a part of a larger workshop package dealing with assertiveness training. It is an initial unit to introduce the concepts of passive, assertive, and aggressive behaviors. It is a 45-minute videotape divided into segments of approximately two minutes each. The videotape presents seven different situations where an assertive

> *response is needed. Each situation is depicted in three versions. The actors are the same in all three versions, but the main character behaves passively, assertively, or aggressively. The specific versions for each situation are arranged in a random order. The situations are also varied so that the interactions are among friends, neighbors, strangers, employers, relatives, clients, and colleagues. While there is no commentary on the characteristics of the three types of behaviors, the examples are so arranged that it is easy to identify consistent behavior patterns related to each type.*
>
> *A printed text which accompanies the protocol material describes the critical attributes of passive, assertive, and aggressive behaviors and instructs the trainee to stop the tape at appropriate places. After each pause, the text provides additional information and instructions on what to watch out for in the next segment.*

Protocol packages for teaching concepts are the major concern of this book. We will provide a detailed analysis of this type of protocol in the third chapter.

6. *Training for an observation system.* A specialized application of protocol packages to teach concepts is the training of observers to use standardized observation systems. In many areas of human interaction, these observation systems and behavioral checklists are used extensively to evaluate interactive performance. For example, in the field of teacher training, there are more than 100 of these observation systems (see Simon and Boyer, 1970) to record different categories of teacher-pupil interactions and objective feedback for teachers' professional development. Here is an example of this application of protocol packages:

Example 6. Stop That or Else. . .

The target population for this protocol is elementary school teachers who will code each other's classroom management behaviors according to the Indiana Behavior Management System (IBMS) (Fink and Semmel, 1971). Briefly, in this system, the coder records what the teacher and the students are doing at ten-second intervals. For example, if the teacher is lecturing and the student is listening to him or her, the observer will code both these behaviors as being "on task." If the student behaves disruptively and if the teacher uses some technique to control him or her, then the observer will record an appropriate category.

The protocol package consists of a self-instructional text which provides paper-and-pencil examples and explanations of each category. After completing this, the teacher trainee works through a fairly long collection of videotape segments containing simulated examples of disruptive behaviors and control techniques. These examples are organized according to the conceptual categories shown in Figures 2 and 3.

Observation systems and checklists for summarizing and describing interactions among people are being used in increasing numbers in other areas in addition to teacher training. Protocol packages have an important role in training people to use these observation devices.

Protocol Packages for Evaluation of Instruction

In addition to the direct instructional uses described above, protocol packages serve a variety of evaluative functions. Here are some applications of protocols for the evaluation of trainees and of training.

Figure 2

Categories of Learner Behavior in IBMS-II
(based on Fink and Semmel, 1971)

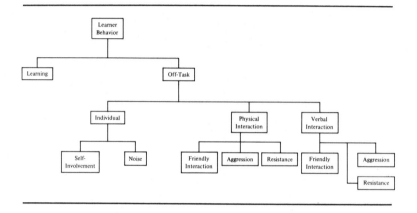

Figure 3

Categories of Teacher Behavior in IBMS-II
(based on Fink and Semmel, 1971)

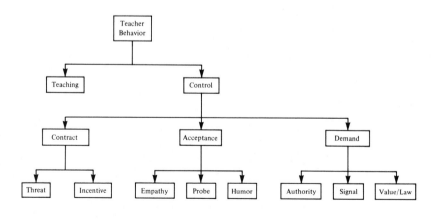

1. *Evaluation of concept mastery.* Earlier we saw how protocol packages can help trainees acquire a conceptual framework. At the end of such training, a good method for checking the trainees' mastery of the concept is to give an application test which involves naturalistic, interactive behaviors portrayed in a protocol form. The trainees are tested for their ability to identify examples of the different concepts in a situation which requires fine discriminations among similar examples. Here is an example of this application of protocol packages:

Example 7. Moral Dilemmas

This is the final test for trainees who have been taught different stages of moral reasoning in children. The protocol test package consists of audiotape recordings of children's responses to a hypothetical moral dilemma. The trainees are to listen to each response and classify it into one of the stages of moral reasoning according to Kohlberg:

1. Punishment-obedience orientation

2. Instrumental-exchange orientation

3. Good boy-nice girl orientation

4. System-maintaining orientation

5. Social-contract orientation

6. Universal ethical-principles orientation

The examples on the tape are selected to vary along different irrelevant dimensions while retaining critical characteristics that identify their membership in a particular category.

---

2. *Evaluation of coder reliability.* In addition to their use in training people to use an observation system, protocol materials are used for checking the reliability of trained coders. Here is an example of this type of evaluative use:

Example 8. Cognitive Demands

This protocol material is used as a test for the trainee's mastery of the Individual Cognitive Demand Schedule (Lynch and Ames, 1971). In this observation system, the questions (and other types of cognitive demands) from the teacher are classified into different types shown in Figure 4.

Figure 4

*Types of Cognitive Demands
(according to Lynch and Ames, 1971)*

LOW LEVEL DEMANDS:
1. Habitual responding ("Repeat after me.")
2. Observing-discriminating ("Say what you see.")
3. Stringing ("Read the first paragraph.")
4. Remembering ("Remember what happened in the story.")

HIGH LEVEL DEMANDS:
5. Explaining (How? Why?)
6. Defining-classifying ("What's a wombat?")
7. Applying-comparing ("What's the difference?")
8. Inferring ("Did the butler do it?")
9. Making believe ("Let's pretend.")
10. Valuing-judging ("Do you think that's nice?")
11. Problem-solving ("How would you fix that?")

The student's response to the question is also coded using the same categories.

The protocol test package consists of a videotape which has three ten-minute segments. Each trainee uses an actual coding sheet and records appropriate catego-

> ries while watching the protocol segments. At the end of
> the session, trainees' codes are compared to a master
> code which has been prepared from a leisurely analysis
> of the segments by experts. The correlation between
> each trainee's record and this master code indicates the
> trainee's reliability.

The most valid test of the trainee's coding performance is the coding of live classroom interaction. However, we do not have a comparison standard unless each trainee is accompanied by an expert coder. The protocol test package may not be the most valid, but it is easy to administer and reliable to score.

3. *Formative evaluation of instruction.* Protocols can also serve as the basis for an evaluation process rather than as a test instrument as in the preceding examples. To understand this application, here is an example of formative evaluation using the concept of protocols:

> ### Example 9. Videotape Microteaching
> Let's assume that we are evaluating a training program for elementary school teachers. This particular course deals with methods of teaching art.
>
> The teacher trainee is required to teach an art lesson to a group of fourth-grade children. A videotape camera records his or her teaching behavior and the children's responses. The unedited protocol tape provides a permanently recallable sample of the teacher's performance. It is systematically analyzed by the supervising teacher to provide formative feedback so that the teacher can improve his or her performance. By incorporating a digital display of time on the videotape, it is possible for the supervising teacher to refer to a specific segment and

> *reinforce or provide correction. The trainee can use the same tape for self-evaluation or share it with a peer for mutual, constructive criticism.*

Audiotape and videotape recordings can be made easily and inexpensively by using currently available equipment. Protocol tapes of a person's performance can be used for professional and personal development. Such evaluation of the trainee's performance can be used not only to improve individual performance, but also to increase the effectiveness of the instruction.

4. *Summative evaluation of instruction.* Just as a final test evaluates if the performance of a trainee is up to prespecified standards, summative evaluation checks if the effectiveness of instruction has reached satisfactory levels. The process of producing protocols can be used for the evaluation of instruction on interactive skills, as in this example:

Example 10. You Have a Right to Remain Silent
Let's assume that our target population is police trainees and that we have developed an extensive course on interrogation techniques. Trainees score high in the final test, but we have to establish that the course produces effective and replicable results. Here is a technique which employs the protocol process for summative evaluation: A standard test situation is set up with a few professional actors (or instructors) playing the roles of suspects. Each player is supplied with a list of different types of behaviors to display during interrogation. A checklist of critical interrogation techniques is also created. Each trainee participates in the role-play situation and interrogates the "suspect." This performance is videotaped, and the tapes are systemati-

> *cally evaluated using the checklist to see if the course resulted in consistent performance to a prespecified standard (such as 80 percent of the trainees demonstrating 80 percent of correct procedures during interrogation).*

Another way of summatively evaluating instruction is to produce protocol tapes of trainees in real-life situations. Producing a protocol tape of on-the-job performance has a major advantage of single-shot observation. The tape can be repeatedly subjected to different types of analysis.

Protocol Packages for Analysis of Instruction

In our last two examples, the protocols have been used much more similarly to the way other social scientists use them—for analysis. Another related use of the protocol process is during the initial analysis stage in instructional development.

1. *Learner and context analyses.* One of the first steps in the design and development of any instructional material is a careful analysis of the needs and the characteristics of the trainees and the context in which the training is to take place. Here is an example of how the production of protocol materials can help in this step.

> ### *Example 11. Back from the Institution*
> *We are a team of instructional developers about to prepare self-instructional packages for mentally retarded adults who are leaving the totally structured environment of a state institution for the more independent situation of a group home. Before producing our instructional materials, we decide to learn more about the characteristics of the learners and the situation in*

> *which they will use the materials. Rather than merely visiting a group home and talking to its residents, we set up video cameras in different rooms of different group homes and produce protocol records of the activities of the residents in their environment. Experts in the area of mental retardation and group homes select the most representative segments from these protocols. We carefully analyze these segments to identify the needs and characteristics of the learners and the resources and constraints in group homes.*

In using protocols in this manner, we lose flexibility and the intensity of a face-to-face on-site analysis. However, we save a significant amount of money and time and obtain a replayable segment of reality which can be shared with various members of the instructional development team.

2. *Task and concept analyses.* While many trainers believe that task and concept analyses should precede the development of a protocol, there is something to be gained by preparing the protocol materials first and then conducting these analyses. Here is an example to illustrate this point:

Example 12. The Inner-City Classroom

Cruickshank (1974) argues for the "situation-first strategy" in the development of protocol materials. In this approach, an educationally significant event is first created. In Cruickshank's example, a film depicts a sixth-grade science class broken into small groups. In one group, a student is swinging a pendulum, another student is keeping time, and still another is recording the time. Sometime during the experiment, the recordkeeper grabs the watch from the timekeeper. The teacher orders him or her to return the watch. The

> *experiment continues. Later, while the teacher is talking to another student, a fight breaks out in the first group. The teacher stops the fight and discovers that the watch is broken . . .*
>
> *After creating a protocol with a significant incident like this, we can check with teachers for authenticity. If it survives careful inspection by the teachers, then a concept analysis is undertaken to discover what is needed to analyze the incident. As examples of concepts related to this incident, Cruickshank lists such concepts as grouping for instruction, experiment, differentiation of labor, reprimand, acquiescence, interruption, and tattling.*

If trainees and experts find a protocol incident to be authentic, and if our task and concept analyses are valid, then our instruction should have a high degree of face validity and relevance.

Summary

In this chapter, we defined a protocol as an authentic, replayable record of interactive behavior in its uninterpreted form, and a protocol package as an instructional design which incorporates a protocol and which is designed to help trainees acquire a framework of interactive behavioral concepts through repeated analyses of the protocol.

Protocol packages contain a protocol component and an instructional component. With very little of the instructional component, we can use the protocol materials to increase the trainees' awareness of an interactive situation. This type of protocol material can also be used as an advance organizer for a complex conceptual framework and as a model for interactive skills. It can provide a stimulus for a group discussion and the sharing of existing conceptual frameworks.

With a larger instructional component, protocol packages can be used for the direct teaching of complex, interactive concepts and the reliable use of checklists and observation systems.

Protocols are used for the evaluation of trainees and training. They are used as stimulus materials for criterion tests of concept mastery and reliable coding. By producing a protocol record of trainees' performances, we can obtain formative and summative evaluation of the effectiveness of instruction.

Protocols are used in the development of instructional materials. Carefully recorded protocols of job and training situations provide us with a base for the analysis and identification of learner needs and characteristics and of the resources and constraints in the training situation. By preparing and checking the authenticity of a protocol depicting a significant incident for the target group, we can create a stimulus for our task and concept analyses.

References

Cruickshank, D.R. The Protocol Materials Movement: One Exemplar of Efforts to Wed Theory and Practice in Teacher Education. *Journal of Teacher Education,* 1974, *25*(4).

Fink, A.H., and Semmel, M.I. Indiana Behavior Management System-II. Bloomington, Indiana: Center for Innovation in Teaching the Handicapped, 1971.

Lynch, W.W., and Ames, A. Individual Cognitive Demand Schedule. Bloomington, Indiana: Center for Innovation in Teaching the Handicapped, 1971.

Simon, A., and Boyer, E.G. (Eds.) *Mirrors for Behavior: An Anthology of Observation Instruments.* Philadelphia: Research for Better Schools, 1970.

Smith, B.O. *et al. Teachers for the Real World.* Washington, D.C.: American Association of Colleges for Teacher Education, 1969.

Thiagarajan, S. *Grouprograms.* Englewood Cliffs, N.J.: Educational Technology Publications, 1978.

II.

OPERATIONAL DESCRIPTION

In the previous chapter, we defined a protocol as *an authentic, replayable record of interactive human behavior in its uninterpreted form* and a protocol package as *an instructional design format which incorporates a protocol and which is designed to teach interactive behavioral concepts.* In this chapter, we first discuss the critical attributes of protocols and protocol packages. We then discuss other attributes of protocol packages which may vary from one example to another.

In the teacher-training literature, a major problem with definitions has been the rigid adherence to the original specification of protocols as *unedited* recordings of *unrehearsed* interactions. This definition presents many problems when we attempt to produce protocol materials with an instructional intent. Logic suggests that a careful selection and systematic sequencing of examples should result in effective and efficient training. However, such an approach violates the critical requirements of a pure protocol. In this book, we sidestep this definitional problem by defining protocols in their pure form and creating a hybrid definition for protocol packages as an instructional design.

Critical Attributes of Protocols

Our definition of protocols implies these four critical characteristics:

1. Protocols are *replayable* recordings.
2. Protocols present *interactive human behaviors.*
3. The behaviors recorded in protocols are *authentic.*
4. Protocols do *not* interpret or explain the recorded behaviors.

Each of these critical attributes is discussed and illustrated below:

1. *Protocols are replayable recordings.* Protocols help us to confront reality. Through our observation of various slices of reality, we recognize different forces at play. This powerful approach to learning has the advantage of providing "live" observation opportunities of interactive events as they take place. In addition to direct observation that allows us a more valid look at reality, protocols—*replayable* recordings—offer other advantages:

• *Reality is transient.* Our limited memory for events limits our ability to analyze and interpret all the elements of our observation. Our memory can sometimes play tricks when we attempt to recall and relate different incidents out of their original sequence. In contrast to this, a videotape record of the same event preserves it in a "permanent" form. Our mental capacities can now focus on the analysis and interpretation of events rather than trying to recall specific details. With the videotape record, we can also resequence the past and relate various incidents in any order.

• *Our sensory capacity is limited.* When we observe a real-life event, our perception is selective. For example, in observing a crowded workshop where a number of small groups are busily discussing various topics, we are selective about what to observe and what to ignore. At a later time, some salient incident may take place in one of the groups which we have been ignoring thus far. Unfortunately, we cannot travel through time and identify the earlier events related to this current incident. With a protocol, we have a replayable record of many things taking place at the same time (although we may not be able to capture *all* of the events in our illustrative incident). In using a protocol, if a current event attracts our attention, it is possible for us to replay the earlier segments to track down relevant factors.

• *Analysis needs verification.* During the observation of real-life incidents, we form hypotheses about various causes and effects. These hypotheses bias our recall of earlier incidents (as has been demonstrated in a number of eyewitness reports). To preserve our objectivity, we should have access to earlier incidents so that we can validate our assumptions. Replayable protocol records permit us to do this.

2. *Protocols present interactive human behaviors.* Many events may be recorded in a replayable form, but we are limiting our definition of protocols to events involving interactive human behaviors. According to this critical attribute, this is an example of a protocol: *a videotape record of a trainee being tutored by an experienced manager*; while this one is *not* an example: *a videotape recording of a trainee working through a computer-assisted instruction lesson on managerial skills*; because the second record does not involve interaction among humans.

In the following pair, the first one is not an example of a protocol because it involves only one human being whereas the second one is an example: (1) *an audiotape recording of a trainee repeating Spanish sentences;* (2) *an audiotape recording of the interaction between the trainees and the instructor in a Spanish classroom.*

The types of interactions that can be recorded as protocols are almost unlimited as can be judged from the variety of examples in the previous chapter. Additional examples may include such interactive behaviors as explaining, interviewing, questioning, quarreling, listening, evaluating, counseling, selling, bargaining, arguing, reinforcing, and all of the infinite variety of behaviors that human beings are capable of exhibiting.

3. *The behaviors recorded in protocols are authentic.* Obviously, a Hollywood version of what is happening during dinner time in a black family is not an authentic protocol; pure protocols record real human interactions rather than scripted portrayals.

It is doubtful if people behave spontaneously when they realize that their behavior is being recorded for posterity. Therefore, can we ever record real human interactions after fulfilling the ethical requirement that participants be informed that their behaviors are being recorded? Nixon's Watergate tapes provide protocols of authentic political interaction at the highest levels of government because they were obtained without the knowledge of most of the participants. However, ethical and economic constraints prohibit us from this approach. After-the-fact confessions as in *Candid Camera* and hidden-camera commercials reduce some of the sneakiness of secret records, but they present complex logistic problems. Fortunately, however, two factors increase the authenticity of human behavior, even after we obtain informed consent for recording them.

• *People adapt fairly rapidly to being recorded.* During the first few days of televising Canadian parliamentary proceedings, most politicians behaved in a self-conscious manner. Within a matter of weeks, however, they became used to the lights and the camera and got immersed in the substance of their own debates. Similar adaptation was reported during the lengthy television recording of *An American Family*, which was broadcast as a PBS series.

• *This adaptation period is speeded up considerably when there are no whirring motors, bright lights, numerous technicians, and bulky equipment.* Recording equipment is becoming more and more unobtrusive. Videotape cameras come in small sizes and can be mounted to blend with the background. They perform without noticeable noise and through remote control. They do not distract the key players in the protocol. In audiotape recorders, what was once limited to cloak-and-dagger espionage is now available for everyone. These silent and camouflaged devices reduce the time required for participants to forget the fact that they are being recorded and to become immersed in what they are doing.

4. *Protocols do not interpret or explain the recorded behaviors.* In their purest form, protocols are not didactic tools. They merely provide the base for analysis and learning rather than heavy-handed teaching of any specific approach to analysis. A travel film which shows how people in a different culture interact with each other *and* explains the cultural significance of this interaction is not a protocol. The explanation is not this obvious in the following nonprotocol recording:

A 15-minute audiotape recording of the sounds in a marketplace of an African village was produced. This recording was edited so that the new version lasted for the same amount of time, but with all interactions in Kru, Kisi, Kpelle, and Mandingo languages arranged in separate clusters.

Even though the edited version does not contain any comments to explain that different segments are in different languages, it is no longer a pure protocol because the editing process has superimposed a specific organizational framework.

The video camera may be an all-seeing eye, but somebody has to point and focus it. Can we ever avoid superimposing our framework on what is being recorded? Probably not, especially in the case of videotape recordings. The director and the cameraperson make a large number of decisions about what to record at any given moment, and these decisions are based on visual and dramatic considerations. To avoid such bias, it is technologically possible for a computer-controlled camera to randomly select different points of view and record videotape segments. However, the resulting lack of continuity will eliminate the advantages of a replayable record.

Critical Attributes of Protocol Packages

Protocols are not efficient and effective instructional tools because, by definition, instruction is goal-based and structured, while protocols are goal-free and unstructured. A pure protocol, however, may be of great use for two other related uses discussed in the previous chapter: They are valid instruments for evaluating instruction and relevant bases for instructional analyses. The ultimate instructional intent of protocol packages is to train people to analyze real-life incidents. A pure protocol reproduces real-life with all its confusing distractions and becomes an ideal item for testing the trainee's ability to apply a conceptual framework to analyze a complex situation. A pure protocol reflects the real-life job situation. An instructional analysis based on this protocol is more likely to identify relevant concepts than an armchair analysis of what concepts the trainee should acquire.

In our discussion above, we faced some problems in maintaining the last two requirements (authenticity of behaviors and unbiased recordings) in a practical context. In defining a protocol *package,* we shall compromise these two ideal attributes to suit our instructional intent and practical realities. The following three critical attributes of a protocol package replace the last two attributes of a pure protocol:

1. Incidents in a protocol package are realistic (but not necessarily real).

2. Incidents in a protocol package are selected to be relevant to its instructional objectives.

3. Incidents in a protocol package are organized to facilitate the learning of a specific conceptual framework.

Figure 5 contains a more complete list of critical attributes for a protocol package. Each of these attributes is briefly discussed and illustrated in the following section.

Figure 5

Critical Attributes of
Protocol Packages

1. *Intents.* Protocol packages are designed to help trainees attain specific instructional objectives.

2. *Contents.* Protocol packages (and their objectives) deal with interactive human behaviors.

3. *Instruction.* Protocol packages include instructional messages and activities.

4. *Format.* Protocol packages contain replayable recordings.

5. *Realism.* Incidents in a protocol package are realistic (but not necessarily real).

6. *Selection.* Incidents in a protocol package are selected to be relevant to its instructional objectives.

7. *Structure.* Incidents in a protocol package are organized to facilitate the acquisition of a specific conceptual framework.

1. *Protocol packages are designed to help trainees attain specific instructional objectives.* These packages are designed to help a group of trainees attain some specific instructional objectives that deal with awareness or analysis of a complex conceptual framework related to human interaction. In this respect, protocol packages differ from pure protocols which are designed to facilitate the creation of new conceptual frameworks.

2. *Protocol packages (and their objectives) deal with interactive human behaviors.* This critical attribute is common to both protocols and protocol packages. Therefore, our previous discussion of this attribute also applies to protocol packages.

3. *Protocol packages include instructional messages and activities.* A pure protocol records what is happening and nothing else. No interpretive comments or instructional messages are added to it. A protocol package contains a number of messages to focus the trainee's attention on specific details of the record and to prompt him or her into identifying critical attributes of a concept.

4. *Protocol packages contain replayable recordings.* This is another critical attribute which is shared by both protocols and protocol packages.

5. *Incidents in a protocol package are realistic (but not necessarily real).* A 15-minute recording of the teacher-pupil interactions in an elementary school classroom will contain so many specific local details that it may not appear real to other teachers in other areas who use other approaches. Because of this, a common experience among early producers of protocol materials has been the "unrealistic" nature of real incidents. The continuum from artificiality to realism is a subjective one, and not enough is known about it. However, it is naive to assume that a real record will always be perceived as realistic.

The producer of a protocol records authentic, unrehearsed human interactions. The producer of a protocol package strives to record a relevant and realistic segment. In doing so, he or she may even use such techniques as scripting and role playing.

6. *Incidents in a protocol package are selected to be relevant to its instructional objectives.* The producer of a pure protocol keeps an open mind and attempts to record reality in its raw form. No specific incident is selected on the basis of predetermined concepts. The camera follows the action which is the most salient to the director or to the cameraperson. By contrast, in a protocol *package,* the incident to be recorded is selected on the basis of some predetermined conceptual framework. For example, if *with-*

drawal is one of the concepts to be portrayed, the cameraperson may focus on a silently sulking participant in a meeting, even though the others may be engaged in a more salient, heated debate over an issue.

7. *Incidents in a protocol package are organized to facilitate the acquisition of a specific conceptual framework.* After recording a number of telephone calls to a counseling service, the producer of a pure protocol does a minimum of technical editing to enhance the intelligibility of the conversations but preserves the chronological sequence. In contrast, let us assume that the producer of a protocol package is interested in helping trainees learn the concepts of reinforcement and·punishment. This producer edits the recordings to isolate clear-cut examples of reinforcing and punishing statements by the counselor. He or she may discard (or store for future use) other segments of the tape and resequence the selected segments so that obvious examples are presented in the beginning and more subtle ones are reserved for the end.

A Comparison of Protocols and Protocol Packages

Protocols and protocol packages share two critical attributes: They are *replayable recordings* of *interactive human behaviors.* They differ in a number of other attributes. A pure protocol aims at presenting a slice of objective reality. Therefore, it records real, unrehearsed events and presents them in an unedited and uninterpreted form. A protocol package aims at helping the learners acquire a conceptual framework to analyze complex human interactions. Because of this instructional intent, a protocol package structures and controls the developmental process and the final product. Thus, a protocol package may contain an instructional explanation in addition to its record of realistic events. Structure during the production of a package is obtained by scripting and prespecifying the incidents to be staged or to be recorded, and by editing the tape to eliminate and resequence the contents.

Because of this control, a protocol package produces more efficient and effective learning than pure protocols. However, these protocols have important roles in the instructional process: Before the development of instruction, they provide a realistic base for appropriate analysis. After instruction, they provide valid tests of the learner's ability to apply the conceptual framework to the analysis of a complex situation.

Variable Attributes of Protocol Packages

The focus of the rest of this book is on protocol *packages.* Our earlier discussion identified seven critical attributes shared by all protocol packages. However, one protocol package may also differ from another in the way in which these critical requirements are met. This section of the chapter discusses the various ways in which protocol packages differ from one another. Variations of protocol packages are listed in Figure 6 in a sequence which parallels the listing of critical attributes in the previous figure.

1. *Variations in intents.* All protocol packages have an instructional intent, and this intent is related to the mastery of a conceptual framework. However, the exact nature of the objective varies from one protocol to another. Based on the examples from the preceding chapter, we may arrange the types of instructional objectives on a continuum which includes the following:

• *Increasing awareness levels.* This is a fuzzy type of objective which requires increased familiarity on the part of trainees with the instructional context. A sample objective of this type is: *Recognize salient dimensions of social interaction in an Indian village.*

Attainment of this objective may be evaluated by asking the trainees for their subjective ratings of familiarity with a novel protocol segment from the same context they have been studying. For example, let us assume that a group which has been through our protocol package rates a novel segment

Figure 6

Variable Attributes of
Protocol Packages

1. *Intents.* Protocol packages may specify different types of awareness and analysis objectives for the instruction.

2. *Contents.* The types of human interactions presented in different protocol packages vary considerably.

3. *Instruction.* The instructional component in the package may be integrated with the protocol component in a number of different ways.

4. *Format.* The protocol packages may use different media (e.g., videotape or audiotape).

5. *Analysis.* The protocol package may be developed with instructional analysis preceding the production of the protocol or *vice versa.*

6. *Development.* Incidents in a protocol package may be scripted and staged, or natural and unrehearsed.

7. *Editing.* The final version of the protocol may be obtained through different amounts of editing.

8. *Continuity.* Incidents presented in a protocol package may be continuous or segmented.

at 3.5 on a five-point scale of familiarity (with one being extremely unfamiliar and five being extremely familiar). If a control group rates the same segment at 1.5 on the same scale, we may consider that the package has produced satisfactory achievement of the instructional objective.

• *Eliciting existing conceptual frameworks.* This instructional objective specifies a purpose for the protocol package. A more operational example follows: *Trainees will volunteer their personal conceptual frameworks for the analysis of the situations presented in the protocol.*

Evaluation of this objective requires observation of a group and recording of the quantity and quality of the analytical comments. We may consider the objectives as being achieved if, for example, after viewing the protocol on shoplifting, each member of a small group enthusiastically participates in the discussion of the segment with relevant analytical comments.

• *Providing advance organizers.* This is another familiarization-type objective dealing with a specific conceptual framework. An example of this type of objective is: *Recognize major conceptual categories related to human interaction in drug counseling.*

Achievement of this objective may be evaluated by asking trainees to list labels for different conceptual categories.

• *Concept acquisition.* This is the major intent of protocol packages. An example of a specific objective in this area is: *Given novel videotaped examples of different types of students' disruptive behaviors and teachers' control strategies, the trainee will be able to correctly classify each example according to the conceptual framework presented in the package.*

Achievement of this objective is evaluated by following the prescription implied in its statement.

• *Coder reliability.* This intent involves mastery of the conceptual framework related to a standardized observation system and its application to the coding of actual interaction. An example of a specific objective in this area is: *Code the cognitive demands made by a trainer and the cognitive levels of the responses given by the trainees.*

Achievement of this objective may be evaluated by the computation of the trainee's reliability in coding. This can be most effectively done by having the trainee code a videotaped segment of instructional interaction and comparing his or her codes with those of master coders. The correlation between these two codings indicates the trainee's reliability.

Protocol packages can be designed to achieve any of these types of conceptual objectives either singly or in various combinations. It is also possible to use the same protocol to help learners achieve different types of objectives by modifying the instructional messages and activities that accompany the protocol.

2. *Variations in contents.* All protocol packages present human interaction. However, the specific nature of this interaction may vary from one protocol to another. A series of protocols in the area of diffusion of innovations, for example, may deal with the interactions between the change agent and the adopter. Within this general framework, however, the exact type of interaction may vary considerably along any of the following dimensions identified in Figure 7. Figure 7 is not a complete list of all possible factors in this domain of human interaction. However, it suggests the hundreds of possible permutations and combinations of specific human interactions. (In the final chapter, we discuss various analytic procedures for identifying and selecting appropriate types of human interactions to be portrayed in a protocol.)

3. *Variations in instruction.* A protocol package consists of two major components: the protocol (examples) and the instruction (rules or concepts). Their interrelationship is discussed in detail in the next chapter; at this time, we may briefly note two dimensions related to their integration.

• *The relationship between protocol and instruction may take the form of discovery learning or didactic exposition.* In the former case, the examples are presented first and, through ingenious questioning, the trainees are encouraged to "discover" the conceptual framework. In the latter case, trainees are presented with the rules (i.e., the conceptual

Figure 7

Variations in the Interactions Between a Change Agent and an Adopter (based on Dormant, 1979)

1. *Type of adopter*: innovators, moderates, resistors, laggards, . . . individuals, groups, systems, . . .

2. *Type of innovation*: simple-complex, concrete-intangible, flexible-rigid, compatible-different, . . .

3. *Type of change agent*: experienced, naive; trained, untrained; authoritative, laissez-faire; . . .

4. *Type of situation*: school, factory, home, office, . . .

5. *Relationship between the adopter and the innovation*: unaware, interested, ready to try out, ready to adopt, ready to institutionalize, . . .

6. *Relationship between the change agent and the innovation*: developed by self, developed by others; enthusiastic, indifferent; . . .

7. *Relationship between the change agent and the institution*: inhouse consultant, outside expert, . . .

8. *Relationship between the institution and the adopters*: hierarchical, equal; controlled, free; voluntary, mandatory; . . .

9. *Type of change agent activity*: getting attention, identifying concerns, answering questions, providing information, promoting discussion, providing demonstration, training, facilitating evaluation, . . .

framework) first and provided with examples later. Combinations of these approaches are possible when a large number of concepts are involved.

• *The protocol and the instruction may either be kept separate or be integrated very closely with each other.* For example, a videotape contains a record of a lengthy client-consultant interaction. Instructions related to the conceptual framework for its analysis are provided in a separate manual. In contrast to this arrangement, another protocol is a self-contained film in the form of an "illustrated lecture." The narrator on the film provides conceptual instruction and illustrates each point with a suitable protocol segment.

4. *Variations in format.* All protocol packages contain replayable recordings, but the media used for these recordings may differ from one protocol to another: audiotape, videotape, and film. Even within a specific class of media, major variations are possible, as in the case of videotape with its different sizes (2-inch, 1/2-inch, 3/4-inch), specifications (reel-to-reel, VHF cassette, Beta format), and color or black-and-white capabilities. (The next chapter discusses media variables in greater detail, while the final chapter suggests a systematic procedure for selecting the most appropriate medium to suit specific instructional objectives, target populations, and training situations.)

5. *Variations in analysis.* An initial step in the systematic development of protocol packages is the concept analysis. However, this analysis may be undertaken at different stages of development. In the "concept-first" approach (Thiagarajan, Semmel, and Semmel, 1974), a major domain of human interaction is identified and analyzed into a conceptual framework. The protocol is produced to reflect this framework. In the "situation-first" approach (Cruickshank, 1974), the script for an authentic protocol is prepared to simulate the types of incidents frequently faced by workers in a specific field. This protocol is produced and revised to

enhance its authenticity. A conceptual framework which is useful for understanding the protocol is identified through an analysis of the protocol itself. The instructional component is produced to reflect this framework.

6. *Variations in development.* The final chapter presents systematic procedures for the design and development of protocol packages. Three approaches are available for producing the protocol component. A protocol videotape of a committee meeting, for example, may be produced through any of these approaches:

• *Recording in a naturalistic setting.* The video camera captures the unrehearsed and authentic performance of the committee in a series of typical meetings.

• *Scripted drama.* A script is produced to illustrate the types of human interactions which are relevant to the instructional objectives. This drama is staged in an appropriate setting using professional or amateur actors. The videotape camera records this production.

• *Structured role play.* This approach lies in between the previous two. In a structured role play, the characters (who could be members of a real committee) are given a general outline of the topics to be discussed and specific suggestions about types of behaviors to demonstrate. Within these guidelines, the actors follow their natural inclinations.

7. *Variations in editing.* The final protocol may have undergone different types and amounts of editing. To continue with our committee meeting example, one producer may record miles of videotape and edit it down to a tight ten-minute sequence. In the process, he or she may rearrange the chronological order of events to suit the conceptual framework. In contrast, another producer may merely record a ten-minute videotape and decide to use it without any editing. Other protocols may fall anywhere between these two extreme cases of editing.

8. *Variations in continuity.* The sequence of one protocol

may differ considerably from another. Here are three different protocols, all of which deal with the same topic of police interrogation and which last for the same amount of time—30 minutes:

The first protocol shows a single episode lasting for the entire 30-minute period. In this episode, we see the same suspect and the same police officer going through the procedure, one step at a time.

The second protocol shows three different vignettes of about ten minutes each. The suspects, police officers, and the crime are different in each vignette. In addition, the officers and the suspects portray different styles of interaction.

The third protocol contains a series of 60-second clips taken from a number of different situations. Because of the rapid changes in the suspects, officers, and the crimes, it is difficult to follow the content of any single clip. However, each clip appears to have a specific conceptual theme. Deliberate contrasts are built between one clip and the next one to emphasize some critical attribute or the range of variations in the same type of behavior.

Summary

All protocol packages have instructional goals dealing with the content of interactive human behavior. They contain a replayable recording accompanied by appropriate instructional messages and activities. Protocol packages select and structure the incidents to facilitate the mastery of a specific conceptual framework. But even while they do so, they attempt to maintain a high degree of realism.

Protocol packages may differ considerably. The specific type of instructional objectives may vary. The process by which they have been produced may also vary. Some protocols begin with the conceptual framework; others, with representative incidents. Some protocols are records of natural interactions, while others present staged action. Some protocols are preserved in their original form, while others are edited drastically. The instructional design of different protocol packages may also vary considerably. Some packages have the instructional messages interwoven with the protocol examples, while others keep them distinctly different. Some packages use film; others use a combination of audiotape and print. Some packages contain a single case study, while others present a rapid succession of short segments.

References

Cruickshank, D.R. The Protocol Materials Movement: One Exemplar of Efforts to Wed Theory and Practice in Teacher Education. *Journal of Teacher and Education,* 1974, *25*(4).

Dormant, D. A Trainer's Guide to Change Agentry. *NSPI Journal,* 1979, *18*(3).

Thiagarajan, S., Semmel, D.S., and Semmel, M.I. *Instructional Development for Training Teachers of Exceptional Children: A Sourcebook.* Reston, Virginia: The Council for Exceptional Children, 1974.

III.

DESIGN FORMAT

This chapter identifies the components of a protocol package and discusses design considerations for each component. The general organization of this chapter reflects the structure of protocol packages as shown in Figure 8. The chapter begins with the separation of the protocol and the instructional components of the package and describes how they are interrelated to each other. This is followed by a discussion of different media which present these components. The protocol component consists of a conceptual domain, superordinate concepts, individual concepts, and critical attributes of these concepts. The scope and sequence of these elements of a protocol are discussed next. The instructional component consists of messages and activities. After explaining and illustrating these elements, the chapter deals with variations in the format of protocol packages which are designed for different types of instructional objectives.

An Overview of the Elements of a Protocol Package

The structure of a protocol package may be analyzed in a number of different ways. One convenient analysis is shown in Figure 8.

At the first level of analysis, we divide the package into *protocol* and *instructional* components. The former is the

Figure 8

Structure of a Protocol Package

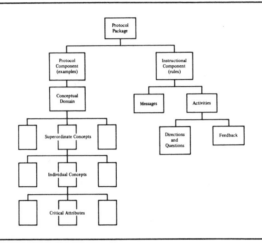

replayable record of interactive behaviors. It is the complete set of examples contained in the package. The instructional component contains all other elements of the package. It includes definitions, descriptions, directions, questions, activities, and feedback.

For example, in a hypothetical protocol package on dealing with husband-wife interaction (based on the work of R.L. Weiss as reported by Gambrill [1977]), the following videotape segments are examples of the *protocol* component:

- *Husband fixes a sloppy hamburger. Wife takes a bite and spits it out.*
- *Husband shaves carefully, takes a shower, dresses neatly, and goes out to meet his wife.*
- *Husband and wife are in bed. Wife is hogging the covers.*

- *Husband pats his wife affectionately. She responds with pleasure.*
- *Husband and wife are discussing a visit by her brother. The conversation becomes a barrage of criticism by husband.*
- *Wife is obviously angry and pouting. Husband asks for the reason. Wife continues her silent treatment.*

The following segments from the same videotape are examples of the *instructional* component:

- *The narrator explains that interactive behavior between a husband and a wife can be classified into **pleases** and **displeases**. Both of these classes of behaviors may occur in such areas as companionship, sex, shared activities, household management, personal habits, and spouse independence.*
- *Superimposed captions at the bottom of the TV screen label the type of interaction taking place (e.g., "Financial Decision-Making: Displease").*
- *Prompting announcements at the beginning of a segment (e.g., "In the following segment, try to identify who is attempting to concentrate and who is distracting. Decide whether this is a **displease** for both people or for only one of them.").*
- *Explanatory comments at the end of a segment (e.g., "All the incidents in the preceding segment contain actions or statements by a spouse that convey acceptance or approval as a person. Therefore, they are all examples of **pleases**.").*
- *Questions and suggested activities (e.g., the screen blanks out and the audio says, "Turn off the videotape recorder and answer the questions on page five of your printed guide.").*

The protocol component of a package is subdivided into one or more levels of superordinate concepts, individual concepts, and critical attributes. The conceptual domain of our sample protocol is *marital interaction.* At the first level, there are two superordinate (higher level) concepts of *pleases* and *displeases.* At the next level, there are two concepts of affectional and instrumental activities. An affectional activity has these three critical attributes:

- directed toward spouse,
- brief duration, and
- acceptance.

This analysis of the protocol component of our hypothetical package on marital interaction is graphically shown in Figure 9. The terminology (of domain, superordinate and individual concepts, and critical attributes) is for analytical purposes only. The actual protocol does not contain these terms; it presents authentic examples of these categories.

The instructional component of the protocol package is subdivided into *messages* and *activities.* The former includes all discussions and definitions which help the learner acquire the conceptual framework. Activities include directions and questions which require the learner to respond in some way. Here are some examples:

- *Listen carefully to the dialogue between wife and husband in the following four segments.*
- *Did all segments deal with the same major area of marital interaction? If they did, what was this area? If they did not, name some of the different areas.*
- *Turn off the tape and write down a list of affectional interactions which you experienced last week.*

The instructional activities also include feedback to evaluate the learner's response. Here are some examples:

Figure 9

Elements of the Protocol Component
(based on the work of R.L. Weiss as
reported by Gambrill [1977])

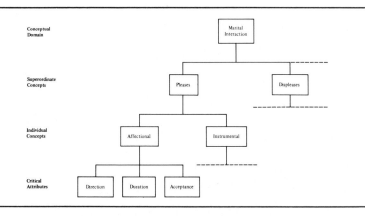

- *The segments dealt with different areas of marital interaction. To be more specific, the set contained at least one example of communication process, shared activities, personal habits, and spouse independence.*
- *Since we do not know what your experiences have been, we cannot give you a set of correct answers. However, you can evaluate your list by taking each item and asking these three questions:*
   1. Was this interaction directed toward you?
   2. Was this interaction brief?
   3. Did this interaction strongly convey acceptance or rejection of you?

Later in this chapter, we discuss specific elements of protocol and instructional components of a package. Before doing that, let us explore the relationships between these two components.

**Relationship Between Protocol
and Instructional Components**

The protocol component presents examples (or illustrations), and the instructional component provides rules. Research on concept learning strongly suggests that both examples and rules are essential and that neither is by itself sufficient. Instruction without illustration results in sterile knowledge. The learner talks knowledgeably about different concepts but is not able to recognize them in real-life situations. This learner provides academically acceptable definitions but does not apply them to analyze relevant interactions. Illustrations without instruction present other dangers and problems. A learner who faces different interactions without classifying them does not acquire generalizable strategies for dealing with them. This learner may produce personal conceptual frameworks and in the process rediscover existing knowledge or create new organizing schemes which are inferior to the available alternatives.

The development of effective and efficient protocol packages requires a careful integration of illustrations with instruction. In other words, it requires a balance between the protocol and instructional components.

There are two major design considerations in integrating these two components into a protocol package.

1. *The question of size*: How large should each protocol-instruction unit be?

2. *The question of sequence*: Should instruction follow the protocol, or should it be the other way around?

There are no definite answers to either of these questions; some tentative prescriptions are suggested in the last chapter. In this chapter, let us discuss the available alternatives.

1. *Size of units.* Figure 10 shows some sample concepts selected from the previous figure. A *large* protocol-instruction unit covers the entire domain. This unit presents all instruction related to marital interaction as a whole and

Figure 10

Sample Concepts at
Different Levels

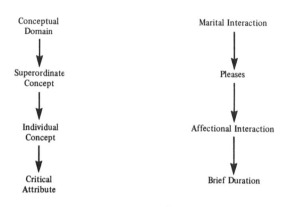

illustrates the conceptual domain through a lengthy protocol
episode. The trainee watches this complex, comprehensive
example without any interruption (or interpretation). In
contrast, a *small* protocol-instruction unit covers a concept
(or a critical attribute of a concept) at the lowest level of
analysis. This miniprotocol segment shows an example of a
brief encounter and follows it up with an instructional
message about the duration of that interaction. This type of
protocol rapidly flipflops between examples and explanations. A *medium-sized* protocol-instruction unit deals with
one cluster or concept at a time, depending upon the number
of levels of analysis.

   No simple formula guides us in the selection of appropriate
unit size. A large unit has the advantage of presenting the entire picture and maintaining the integrity of the concepts. It
has the disadvantage of frustrating the learner in acquiring
the concept and in applying it to real-life situations. A small

unit has its own advantages and limitations: The concept is easier to acquire and apply, but very few real-life situations can be usefully analyzed at this molecular level.

The choice of the appropriate unit size depends on a number of factors, including the nature of the instructional objective and the complexity of the concept. Another important factor is the level of the learner: A large unit for one learner could be a small one for another.

2. *Sequence.* After we have selected the appropriate unit size, we are faced with the sequencing question. Within each unit, which should come first: protocol or instruction? Let us discuss the alternatives available in answer to this question.

Considerable research was done in this area in the early days of programmed instruction. Programmers referred to the illustrations as *egs* (for examples) and the instructions as *ruls* (for rules) and debated on the merits of *egrul* vs. *ruleg* sequences. No definite answer came out of this research because the choice of sequence depends upon the complexity of the concept, the level of the learners, the nature of the instructional objectives, and a number of other factors. However, the debate resulted in two alternatives (and a number of variations) to the sequencing question.

A *ruleg* sequence is didactic in nature. It begins with an explanation of the conceptual framework. Then, it presents examples to illustrate this definition.

Here is an example of the *ruleg* sequence:

> *The videotape on marital interactions opens with a minilecture by the narrator: "A wife and a husband interact with each other in many different ways. In the present segment, we explore a special type of these interactions which are called affectional interactions. All affectional interactions have three things in common. They are directed toward the other, they are brief, and*

> *they strongly convey acceptance or rejection of the spouse."*
>
> *This is followed by a number of illustrations of affectional interactions:*
>
> *Husband is yelling at wife for smoking.*
>
> *Wife greets husband affectionately when he returns home from the office.*
>
> *Wife interrupts husband's nagging by screaming, "Shut up!"*
>
> *Husband brings a cup of coffee to wife.*

The same *ruleg* approach can be used with larger protocol-instruction units:

> *This version begins with a discussion of the conceptual domain: First, the concept of marital interaction is defined and discussed. This is followed by the identification and definition of instrumental and affectional interactions. Finally, the critical attributes of affectional interactions are discussed. After all of this, a fairly lengthy protocol episode between a husband and a wife is shown. This episode contains examples of different types of marital interactions.*

Finally, the *ruleg* approach can be applied to a smaller protocol-instruction unit, as in this example:

> *The narrator on the screen says, "Most interactions between husbands and wives are very brief. Watch the following interactions." This is followed by a rapid series of protocol clips which last for less than ten seconds*

> *each. The narrator returns and says, "Notice that all of*
> *these interactions are directed against each other." The*
> *same series is replayed. The narrator returns once more*
> *and says, "Some of the interactions strongly convey*
> *approval of the other person. Here are some examples."*
> *Another instant replay, but this time only the positive*
> *clips . . .*

Let us now look at the opposite sequence—the *egrul*. This sequence involves discovery learning. A number of examples are presented first. The definition is derived from these examples.

Here is an example of an *egrul* sequence in the same conceptual domain:

> *The videotape begins with a series of illustrations of*
> *positive and negative affectional interactions between a*
> *husband and a wife. At the end of this segment, the nar-*
> *rator explains that all the examples contained three crit-*
> *ical attributes and identifies them. He or she then supplies*
> *the label* **affectional interaction** *for the concept.*

The same *egrul* sequence can be applied to smaller and larger protocol-instruction units. Also, many variations of these two basic types are possible. For example, a *rulegrul* sequence begins with the definition of the concept, illustrates it with examples, and reviews the definition. An *egruleg* sequence presents examples, derives the definition, and strengthens it with additional examples.

Most of the above examples appear to be inefficient because we created them to illustrate two types of sequences. You should not use these examples as models for the development of your own protocol packages. One obvious cause of inefficiency in these examples is the passive role assigned to the learner. Active participation in the learning process is a highly desirable requirement for concept learning, and it is easily achieved by providing either the *rul* or the *eg* and requiring the learner to supply the other. And this can be done in both *ruleg* and *egrul* sequences.

Here are some examples which are labeled with *ruls* and *egs* to indicate the rules and examples to be supplied by the learners.

1. *egrul*:

> *The tape shows a series of examples of interactions between different couples. The narrator asks a series of questions: "What were the common elements in all interactions which you observed? Think for a moment . . . What do you remember about the duration of each interaction? . . . Was there someone other than the husband and wife in each interaction? . . . Would you say that all interactions showed an acceptance or rejection of the spouse? . . . After a suitable pause, the narrator provides appropriate feedback to these questions.*

2. *ruleg*:

> *The narrator defines the concept of affectional interactions. He or she then says: "I am sure that even if you have only been married for a few days, you have already experienced a number of these affectional interactions. Take a moment now to write down some examples of these interactions which you remember." After a suitable pause, the narrator provides feedback by reviewing*

> *the critical attributes of the concept and asking the*
> *trainees to check their list to make sure that each item*
> *has all the critical attributes.*

3. *egruleg*:

> *The tape shows a number of examples of marital inter-*
> *action. The narrator explains that they are all examples*
> *of affectional interactions and identifies the three criti-*
> *cal attributes. He then asks the trainees to supply more*
> *examples from their own experiences.*

These are just a few of the various sequences where the trainee can actively participate in the instructional process.

Media

All examples and rules in a protocol package may be presented through a variety of media—audiotape, print, slide, filmstrip, overhead transparency, 16mm film, Super-8 filmloop, videotape, and CAI terminals.

Should the protocol component and the instructional component be produced in the same medium or different media? Before we answer this question, perhaps we should discuss a prior one: How do we select the most appropriate medium (or combination of media) for protocol and instructional components?

A practical article by Stolovitch (1977) has reduced the media selection process to a systematic procedure. In his article, Stolovitch identifies four classes or requirements that influence the selection of a suitable medium (see Figure 11). These requirements are to be matched against the attributes of different media (rather than vague labels for the medium) to select a suitable combination.

Figure 11

*Requirements for Instructional Media
(based on Stolovitch [1977])*

CONTENT REQUIREMENTS:	PRODUCTION REQUIREMENTS:
Reproduction of sound	Ease of editing
Reproduction of visuals	Ease of transporting equipment
Motion	Simplicity of use
Color	Cost constraints
Three-dimensionality	Speed of production
Realism	
TRAINEE REQUIREMENTS:	**DISTRIBUTION REQUIREMENTS:**
Acceptance of trainees' responses	Ease of editing
Feedback to trainees	Flexibility of scheduling
Auditory explanations	Availability of hardware
Visual explanations	Ease of use
Self-pacing	Inexpensive cost
Random access	Flexibility of grouping
	Ease of set-up
	Compactness

The contents of the protocol packages deal with human interaction which involves a large proportion of verbal exchanges. Is it possible to use the *print* medium to present this verbal interaction and also to gain other advantages? Can we transcribe the major elements of the interaction as in the example below (from Lynch and Ames, 1971)?

Teacher: *Now this is what we're going to do in the game today. And I hope that we have good thinkers and people who can make good sentences. I am going to say a word, or maybe even two words, and I want you to tell me whether you would say hearing, feeling, smelling, tasting, or seeing. Now listen to the first one: I am going to say "chocolate candy cooking." Then I will call someone and you will say "I can SMELL chocolate candy cooking." Could you feel chocolate candy cooking? No, it would be too hot to touch. But you could smell chocolate candy cooking. Okay. I'm going to take turns from one team to the other. Okay? Get set now. Could you say a correct sentence for me? Now be careful, and I hope you answer in a good sentence. Now I will say the word, and you answer: I can SMELL or I can TASTE or I can HEAR or whatever it is. Now let's start with Ricky. Now Ricky's going to listen. "A radio playing."*

Ricky: *A radio playing. I can hear it.*

Teacher: *All right . . . Now just say "I can hear a radio playing."*

Ricky: *I hear a radio . . .*

Teacher: *I can hear . . .*

Ricky: *I can hear a radio playing.*

> *Teacher:* Okay. You don't smell a radio playing, do you, you HEAR a radio playing. Here's one for Judy. "A red-hot iron."
>
> *Judy:* For ironing the clothes.
>
> *Teacher:* What would **you** do with a red-hot iron, Bobby?
>
> *Bobby:* I'd drop it. (Giggles)
>
> *Teacher:* What would you do, Harold?
>
> *Harold:* I'd .. uh .. iron clothes.
>
> *Teacher:* Do you .. touch it, do you smell it, do you taste it, do you see it, or do you hear it? Red team?
>
> *Carol:* I can see a red-hot iron. (Mumbles)
>
> *Teacher:* Now say it in a nice voice.
>
> *Carol:* I can see a red-hot iron.
>
> *Teacher:* A point for the red team! Now . . . Jimmy. "A ham sandwich and a pickle."

This printed transcript records the verbal elements of the interaction between a first-grade teacher and her class. It is a simple and inexpensive medium. However, it violates a major requirement (perhaps *the* major requirement) for the protocol component: *realism*. Protocol materials should have a high level of authenticity; much gets lost in the translation of the dynamic classroom interactions into the static script.

For example, the tone of one's voice plays a significant role in human interaction. Depending upon the tone, the teacher's statement, "All right . . . Now just say 'I can hear a radio playing,' " can indicate concern, exasperation, frustration, sarcasm, or just plain feedback. The script may indicate some types of emphasis through underlining and parenthetical comments, but this involves an inference (rather than presenting a piece of reality and letting the learner make his or her own inference).

An audiotape recording increases the degree of realism because it captures the tone of the speaker's voice and other nonverbal noises (such as mumbling and giggling) during the interaction. However, as much as 80 percent of the meaning in human communication is reportedly derived from such visual cues as eye contact, body posture, facial expression, and spatial relationships. Audio recordings suffer from enormous limitations.

An effective medium for the protocol component combines visual and auditory recording capabilities. This brings us to film or videotape. In terms of production considerations, videotapes are easier and faster to produce than films. In terms of distribution considerations, 16mm projectors are more widely available (especially in educational institutions) than videotape recorders. There is also a compatibility problem among the different formats of videotapes available today. However, this situation is rapidly changing. Within a few years, videotape recorders are more likely to be available in both educational and training situations—and even in homes!

Thus, it appears that the most appropriate medium for the protocol component is the videotape. Does this mean that audiotape and print have no place in a protocol package? This conclusion does not necessarily follow, since we have not discussed the most appropriate medium for the instructional component. Even for the protocol component, audiotape recordings may be all we need (and they could even be more realistic) in certain types of human interactions. Here are some hypothetical examples:

- *A protocol of interactions between a counselor and the client over the telephone. (The package deals with nondirective counseling.)*
- *A protocol of interchanges among truck drivers using CB radio. (The package deals with violations of FCC Regulations.)*

> - *A protocol of interchanges between the host of a late-night radio talk show and people who call him or her on the telephone. (The package deals with types of questions.)*

Although this is stretching our imagination a little bit, it is possible to have a *print* protocol reflect the following types of human interaction:

> - *A portfolio of complaint letters to a big corporation and the responses. (The package deals with types of complaints that get results.)*
> - *A collection of questionnaires and typical returns from respondents. (The package deals with strategies of questionnaire construction.)*
> - *A sheaf of memos and replies from different departments of a Federal agency. (The package deals with writing styles.)*

Authenticity is the most critical requirement for the protocol component, while *control* is the most critical requirement for the instructional component. A protocol should contain all the irrelevant distractors from real life to train people to analyze real-life situations. But during the instructional process, we may approach this level of realism gradually so as not to frustrate or frighten the learners in the beginning. To focus the learners' attention on the verbal portion of an example, we may use an audiotape recording or a printed transcript. Actually, print is the most flexible and cost-effective medium for instructional purposes, when we consider the following requirements for concept teaching (based on such sources as Clark [1971] and Merrill and Tennyson [1977]):

- A list of definitions which is permanent and easy to use.
- *Simultaneous* presentation of different examples to permit comparisons among them.
- Opportunity to study and analyze the example and to attend to different elements of it.
- Provision for self-selected review of examples presented earlier.
- A permanent list of concept labels.
- Opportunity for the trainee to provide written responses to questions.

All of these requirements can be inexpensively and elegantly met through print, which provides the control and flexibility needed by the instructional designer (and the learner).

We do not prescribe videotapes for all protocol components and print for all instructional components. We may describe the ideal media combination for a protocol package in the following terms:

- Unless the domain of human interaction exclusively involves written documents or auditory messages, videotape is the most suitable medium for presenting authentic protocol components.
- Less complex and more permanent examples may be presented for instructional purposes in printed scripts.
- Instructional messages are presented primarily through print. This is especially appropriate for messages which have to be saved for future reference (e.g., a glossary of technical terms).
- Instructional activities may be presented either through the videotape or by referring the trainee to a printed manual. You should choose the least disruptive medium at that point.

Scope of the Protocol Component

With our understanding of the relationship between the two components of the protocol packages, we are now ready to discuss in detail the design format of each component.

The major concern in the design of the protocol component is the portrayal of concepts (Hudgins, 1971). The design format of the protocol component may be analyzed with the aid of principles and procedures for concept analysis (Markle and Tiemann, 1970; Tiemann and Markle, 1978).

As Tiemann and Markle (1978) point out, there is a surprising "fuzziness" in the way different people interpret the term "concept," primarily because they treat it as being synonymous with "idea." Therefore, before getting into our discussion, let us make sure that we have a shared concept of "concept."

A concept is a unit of stimulus events which elicits a single response. Each unit has key properties which make us include it in a specific class. At the same time, there are differences among the stimuli.

A simple example will make our definition more concrete and easier to understand. The key properties of the concept *square* are four sidedness, equal sidedness, flatness, enclosure of an area, and right-angled nature of the corners. Every time we come across a figure with these key properties, we include it in the class of *squares*. We do this even when the examples of squares differ in any property other than the key ones: small or big, black or white, straight or tilted.

The key properties which define membership in a concept class are called *critical attributes*. Other properties whose variations do not affect the membership in the concept class are called *variable attributes*. With the abstract concepts in the domain of human interaction, it is difficult to isolate and to recognize critical and variable attributes. However, as we see from the frequent examples in this book, it can be done.

Protocol packages often deal with a number of concepts, and therefore it is important to understand the relationship between different concepts. Most of the concepts in a protocol can be arranged into a hierarchy. At the top of this hierarchy is the broadest concept which defines a domain of human interaction such as *classroom interaction*. This higher-level (superordinate) concept can be analyzed into lower-level (subordinate) concepts as shown in Figure 12.

In a conceptual hierarchy, all concepts at one level also belong to the superordinate concept classes above it. Thus, *teacher behavior* is a type of *classroom interaction; control* is a type of *teacher behavior; demand* is a type of *control; value/law* is a type of demand. An example of any subordinate concept is also an example of all superordinate ones in the hierarchy. Thus, this statement is an example of value/law:

> *"Mary, you know that we don't disturb our neighbors during independent study."*

It is also an example of all superordinate concepts in this hierarchy: *demand, control, teacher behavior,* and *classroom interaction.*

Within the same level of the hierarchy, one concept is said to be coordinate to another. For example, *threat* and *incentive* are coordinate concepts (since both of them are at the same level—one level below *contract*). An example of a concept is not an example of its coordinate concepts. For example, this is an example of *threat*:

> *If you two don't stop talking, I'm going to make you stay in during recess.*

This is an example of *incentive*:

> *If you two stop talking and pay attention for the rest*

Figure 12

Hierarchy of Classroom Interaction Concepts

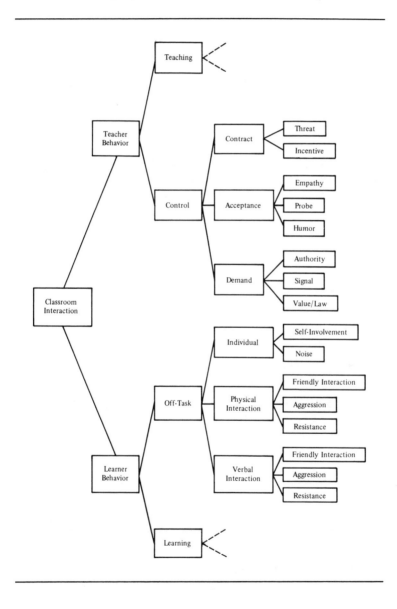

> *of the period, I'll let you be the group leaders during our game session this afternoon.*

The example of *threat* is not an example of *incentive* (and vice versa). (However, both of these are examples of *contract* which is the superordinate concept.)

The critical attributes of *contract* are the following:

- The teacher makes a deal with the off-task student.
- The deal specifies the off-task behavior.
- It also specifies a consequence.

The critical attributes of *threat* are the following:

- The teacher makes a deal with the off-task student.
- The deal specifies the off-task behavior.
- It specifies a consequence if the student continues the off-task behavior.
- The consequence is punishment.

The critical attributes of *incentive* are the following:

- The teacher makes a deal with the off-task student.
- The deal specifies the off-task behavior.
- The deal requires the student to stop the off-task behavior.
- The deal specifies a consequence.
- The consequence is a reward.

By comparing the critical attributes of the concepts of *contract, threat,* and *incentive,* we discover the following:

- The number of critical attributes increases as we get lower in our hierarchy. *Threat* (and *incentive*) have more critical attributes than *contract* has.

- The critical attributes for a concept include the critical attributes for all of its superordinate concepts in the same hierarchy. Thus, the three critical attributes for *contract* are also critical attributes for its subordinate concepts. And although we did not make these explicit, *threat* (or *incentive*) should also have these critical attributes from the higher levels of the hierarchy:

- It is a noninstructional activity.
- It is a teacher behavior.
- It takes place in the classroom.

Types of Example

Analysis of concepts at different levels suggests the scope of examples for the protocol component of a package. Usually, the package focuses on one convenient level of concepts and refers to the superordinate levels as and when necessary. Frequently, the superordinate concepts may be assumed to be a part of the trainee's entry-level knowledge. A protocol package on classroom management, for example, may deal directly with the lowest row of Figure 12 and assume that the trainees already have a good understanding of the teacher and learner behaviors, classroom behaviors, and perhaps even contract, acceptance, and demand.

The examples in this protocol focus on the bottom level of the hierarchy. What types of example and how many of them should we use? The number and nature of examples depend upon the attributes of a concept. Let's take another concept class—this time from learner behavior—to illustrate this point.

This is a positive example of the concept *physical aggression*:

John is biting Joe's thumb.

This is a negative example (or, as we prefer to call it, *nonexample*) of the concept:

John and Joe are talking excitedly about the baseball game.

The example includes *all* the critical attributes of the concept. The nonexample lacks *at least one* critical attribute. To check if our example is really an example, we need to identify the critical attributes of physical aggression:

- It involves a physical interaction.
- It is hostile.
- It involves other people.

We see that the example of John biting Joe's thumb possesses all three critical attributes. The nonexample lacks two critical attributes: It does not involve physical interaction, and it is (or at least appears to be) friendly in nature.

The concept of physical aggression has some variable attributes also:

- *Provocation.* Physical aggression may be self-initiated or provoked by someone else's behavior.

- *Target of aggression.* The person against whom the physical aggression is directed may be another student, the teacher, or anyone else.

- *Form of aggression.* Physical aggression may be in the form of kicking, pushing, slapping, biting, or punching. (It does not even require actual physical contact: Throwing a chair at the teacher is an example.)

- *Verbal accompaniment.* The act of physical aggression may or may not be accompanied by verbal abuse.

Both common sense and experimental studies suggest that examples should show a wide range of variations to help the trainee generalize to a wide range of real-life situations. Very often, because of convenience, all examples in a protocol may accidentally have the same variable attribute and thus encourage undergeneralization of the concept. For example, if all our examples show boys as the aggressors and girls as victims, we may contribute to an unnecessary stereotype and restrict the understanding of the concept.

The nature and number of examples in a protocol should be sufficient to cover the entire range of variable attributes.

Markle and Tiemann (1970) suggest elegant techniques for using the smallest number of examples and, at the same time, ensuring the widest divergence. In the case of physical aggression, the suggested range of examples is given in Figure 13.

Figure 13

*Range of Examples of **Physical Aggression***

Irrelevant Attribute	Range of Examples Suggested
Provocation	An *unprovoked* attack.
	A *retaliatory* fight.
Target of aggression	One student fighting with *three others.*
	Student fighting with *teacher's aide.*
Form of aggression	Student *kicking* another student.
	Student *throwing a book* at the teacher.
Verbal accompaniment	Student *screaming,* "I'll kill you!" as he or she rushes toward the teacher.
	Student *silently* choking his or her opponent in a fight.

Types of Nonexample

A wide range of examples ensures effective generalization

of a concept. However, it does not ensure the necessary discriminations between examples and nonexamples. Without such discriminations, a trainee may mistake a friendly boxing match for an example of physical aggression. To avoid the error of overgeneralization, Markle and Tiemann (1970) suggest the use of nonexamples.

Anything which is not an example of a concept is a nonexample of it. For example, flying a kite on a lovely spring day is a nonexample of physical aggression. However, this is such a way-out nonexample that it has no instructional value when included in a protocol dealing with physical aggression. In contrast to this, take the nonexample of the *friendly* boxing match between two students. It includes all the required critical attributes of physical aggression except one. It includes the attributes of *physical nature* and *involvement of others;* it lacks one—and only one—*hostility.* Such a nonexample (which is called a *close-in* nonexample) provides opportunities for the trainee to learn fine discriminations by making them. (Close-in nonexamples belong to the same conceptual hierarchy and are examples of coordinate concepts.)

The nature and number of nonexamples for a protocol are suggested by the critical attributes of the concept. We need to use at least one (preferably more than one) nonexample which lacks one (and only one) of the critical attributes. Figure 14 lists a suggested set of nonexamples for the concept of *physical aggression.*

Summary of the Scope of the Protocol Component

Some key design considerations from our discussion of the scope of the protocol component are summarized below:

• The selection of examples should be based on a systematic analysis of the concepts from the selected domain of human interaction.

• A hierarchy chart helps us to organize the concepts systematically and to identify relationships among them.

Figure 14

Nonexamples of the Concept of
Physical Aggression

Critical Attribute	Nonexample in Which This Attribute Is Missing
Physical nature	Student verbally insulting the teacher.
Hostility	An accidental push in line.
Involvement of others	Student banging his or her head against the wall.

• The protocol package focuses on the lowest level in the concept hierarchy. Higher levels of the hierarchy contain broader concepts which are likely to be within the trainee's existing level of knowledge.

• We need divergent examples to help the trainee generalize the concept to a wide range of real-life situations. The range of examples is suggested by the variable attributes of the concept.

• We also need close-in nonexamples to help the trainee acquire the necessary discriminations. These close-in nonexamples are suggested by the critical attributes of the concept.

Scope of the Instructional Component

The protocol component of a package provides examples of related concepts. The instructional component helps the trainee to acquire the conceptual framework and to apply it to real-life situations.

Before exploring the scope of the instructional component, let us briefly discuss its objective. Different types of instructional objectives may be applied to conceptual content (Clark, 1971). The three major types of objective related to protocol packages are given below, along with a sample test item used to measure the attainment of each objective:

Type 1. Memorization
Objective: The trainee will be able to correctly define concepts related to teacher control of disruptive behaviors.
Sample test item: List all major types of teacher control techniques used in the classroom and define each technique.

Type 2. Classification
Objective: Given real or simulated incidents from a classroom, the trainee will be able to correctly classify examples of disruptive student behaviors and teacher control techniques into appropriate concept categories.
Sample test item: You are about to view a 15-minute videotape segment of classroom interactions. At different times during this segment, an audio tone will sound. At each tone, write down the concept names for the behaviors of the student and the teacher.

Type 3. Generation
Objective: In a real or simulated classroom situation, the trainee will demonstrate specific behavior control techniques.
*Sample test item: Conduct a microteaching lesson on social studies for 15 minutes. Your peers (who will play the role of fourth graders) have been instructed to disrupt the lesson from time to time. When they do so, use **empathic control** and **humor** to bring them back to task.*

While a protocol package may be used to achieve any of these types of objective, the first one is too trivial for this instructional design format. You can help your trainees achieve memorization objectives more efficiently (and less expensively) by giving them a list of definitions and having them memorize it. The third type of objective is too complex for a protocol package. Although a basic understanding of classroom management concepts will facilitate the achievement of this objective, such understanding is not sufficient. Additional instruction and practice are required before the trainee will be able to fluently demonstrate the required behavior.

Protocol packages are most suited for the second type of objective, which requires classification behavior. While the type of action specified in the third objective is the ultimate goal of any worthwhile instruction in the domain of human interaction, action without analysis is an undesirable outcome. Protocols provide an analytical base upon which effective and informed action can be built. And this is the major rationale provided by Smith and his colleagues (1969) in their original plea for protocol materials in teacher training.

Instructional Messages

The type of instructional objective for a protocol package helps us to specify the scope of the instructional component. As we indicated earlier, this instructional component consists of messages and activities.

Instructional messages. The protocol component provides examples, and the instructional messages analyze and interpret them. One type of message provides the terminology related to the concept. This includes:

• Name of the concept (e.g., *threat, incentive, empathic control,* and *humor*).

• Critical attributes of the concept [e.g., *empathic control* is (a) a statement by the teacher (b) indicating an understanding of the student's feelings (c) when no other control is being used].

• Identification of the superordinate concepts (e.g., empathic control is a *teacher control* behavior).

• Definition. (This usually identifies the superordinate concept and lists the critical attributes. For example, *physical aggression* is an off-task learner behavior [superordinate concept] which involves a hostile physical interaction with someone else [critical attribute].)

Another type of instructional message helps the learner focus on various properties of the example and to differentiate between its critical and variable attributes. This type of instructional message is called *attribute isolation.*

Attributes can be isolated through the use of verbal and nonverbal prompts. Here are some examples of attribute isolation of *physical aggression* through the use of *verbal* prompts:

Auditory commentary: The videotape presents an example of physical aggression in the classroom. Near the end of the incident, the sounds from the location are subdued as the narrator comments: "Did you notice that John became angry because he was provoked by Joe? John's attack on Joe is in retaliation to Joe's hostile name-calling."

Captions: The videotape shows an act of physical aggression in the classroom. While the sights and sounds of this incident are being presented, captions appear on the bottom of the screen. These terms remain on the screen for the appropriate period of time: "Physical act," "Hostile," "Directed toward someone else."

Textual commentary: A printed booklet in the protocol package contains introductory instructions. These include viewing notes to be read before the presentation of each segment. These notes prompt the trainee to watch for specific attributes:

*"During the first few minutes of this segment, you will see a number of incidents of physical aggression. As you watch them, pay particular attention to the **causes** of the aggressive behavior."*

Here are some examples of attribute isolation through the use of *nonverbal* prompts:

Closeup: *The videotape presents an act of physical aggression in the classroom. At the climactic juncture, the physical nature of the interaction is emphasized by a closeup shot of a punch on the victim's nose.*

Freeze frame: *The videotape shows a scene of mounting tension in the classroom. Angie has just hit Sue in the back of the head with her purse. The teacher looks at Angie and says, "Careful, Angie, you might hurt your purse!" Angie, Sue, and the rest of the class start laughing. The action on the television screen stops at this juncture to highlight the laughter, which is a critical attribute of **humor** as a control technique.*

Instant replay: *The videotape has presented a series of examples of **noise** as a disruptive behavior. In the current scene, students are performing an experiment in the chemistry lab. Dan picks up a beaker with some purple solution. The beaker is obviously hot. Dan screams and drops it. The beaker shatters to pieces with a loud crash. The action stops, and the scene is replayed to emphasize that the scream and the noise are not intentional. (Because they are not intentional, the noise is not disruptive.)*

Instructional activities. Another effective way of isolating an attribute is to have the trainee do something with it. Active participation is an effective learning strategy, not only for emphasizing an attribute, but also for all other aspects of concept acquisition. By asking questions and requiring relevant activities in the instructional component, we can increase the probability that the trainee will effectively apply the concepts to real-world situations.

Different types of questions and activities are useful at different stages of instruction. In the initial stages, for example, we may ask the trainee to recognize the presence of a critical attribute or repeat the name of the concept. In the final stages, we may require him or her to make critical discriminations among examples of very similar concepts which are presented as authentic protocols.

In general, all instructional activities provide some information to the trainee and ask for something else in return. Figure 15 classifies different types of instructional activities from a protocol package.

Feedback

Questions encourage the trainee to actively participate in the instructional process. After the trainee provides a response, we need to provide some form of feedback to evaluate this response. By comparing the feedback with the response, the trainee can correct any error or confirm the answer.

When the question calls for the name of the concept, the feedback is the single, correct name for the concept. Since our objective is to strengthen the proper use of the terminology, we do not permit variations to this answer. However, when we ask for a definition or a list of critical (or variable) attributes, we are more interested in the meaning of the trainee's response than in the exact wording or sequence. Here are some sample questions of this type and appropriate feedback:

Figure 15

*Types of Instructional Activities
from a Protocol Package*

Information given to the trainee	Response required from the trainee
Name of the concept	• Definition of the concept • List of critical attributes • Examples of the concept • Name of a superordinate (or subordinate or coordinate) concept
Definition of the concept	• Name of the concept • Examples of the concept
List of critical attributes	• Name of the concept • Examples of the concept
Examples of the concept	• Name of the concept • Definition of the concept • List of critical attributes • List of variable attributes
Nonexamples of the concept	• Identification of missing critical attribute(s)
Name of two concepts	• Nature of relationship (e.g., superordinate, subordinate, or coordinate) between them
Examples of different concepts	• Classification into correct concept categories

---

Question: What is **noise**?

Feedback: Your response may be in your own words, but it should contain the following points:

    a. It is an off-task student behavior.

    b. It is intentional (not accidental).

    c. It distracts other students from their task.

    d. It does not involve interaction with others.

Question: Recall the last three segments on the video-tape program. Write down a list of common elements in the three incidents.

Feedback: Here are some of the key elements you might have noticed:

    1. Two people are talking to each other.

    2. The topic of the conversation is unrelated to the topic of the lesson.

    3. The tone of the conversation is friendly.

(You need not have used the same words in your response. Also, the order in which you listed them may be different.)

Sometimes your question may call for an open-ended response. Here are some suggested methods for providing feedback:

Question: List the major student and teacher behaviors in the episode you just saw.

Feedback: The videotape replays the episode. The trainee is asked to check his or her list against the actual incidents and to identify any missing or imagined items.

Question: Recall your classroom days and list three

examples of conditioned stimuli used by your teachers for behavior management.

Feedback: Check each item in your list to make sure that it contains the following critical attributes of a conditioned stimulus.

   a. It is used to control disruptive behavior.
   b. It lasts for a very brief period of time.
   c. Students recognize it as a signal to stop their misbehavior.

Usual examples of conditioned stimuli include pointing, snapping fingers, pause in speech, staring, calling the student's name, and "Sh!"

Summary of the Scope of the Instructional Component

Figure 16 provides a visual summary of the different parts of the instructional component and their interrelationships.

References

Clark, D.C. Teaching Concepts in the Classroom: A Set of Teaching Prescriptions Derived from Experimental Research. *Journal of Educational Psychology,* 1971, *62*(3).

Gambrill, E.D. *Behavior Modification: Handbook of Assessment, Intervention, and Evaluation.* San Francisco: Jossey-Bass, 1977.

Hudgins, B.B. The Portrayal of Concepts: An Issue in the Development of Protocol Materials. In *Acquiring Teaching Competencies: Reports and Studies.* Bloomington, Indiana: Center for the Development of Training Materials in Teacher Education, 1971.

Lynch, W.W., and Ames, C. *Individual Cognitive Demand Schedule.* Bloomington, Indiana: Center for Innovation in Teaching the Handicapped, 1971.

Figure 16

*Parts of the Instructional Component
and Their Interrelationships*

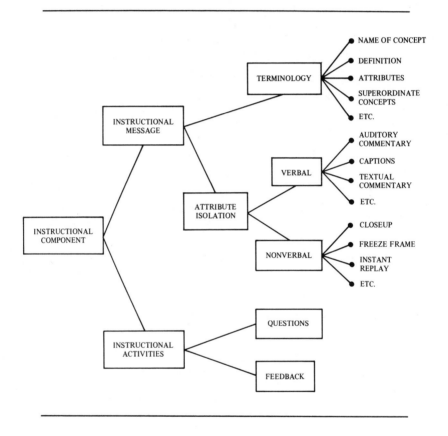

Markle, S.M., and Tiemann, P.W. *Really Understanding Concepts, or in Frumious Pursuit of the Jabberwock.* Champaign, Illinois: Stipes, 1970.

Merrill, M.D., and Tennyson, R.D. *Teaching Concepts: An Instructional Design Guide.* Englewood Cliffs, New Jersey: Educational Technology Publications, 1977.

Smith, B.O. *et al. Teachers for the Real World.* Washington, D.C.: American Association of Colleges for Teacher Education, 1969.

Stolovitch, H.D. Systematically Selecting Media: A Mathematical Procedure. *NSPI Journal,* 1977, *16*(7).

Tiemann, P.W., and Markle, S.M. *Analyzing Instructional Content: A Guide to Instruction and Evaluation.* Champaign, Illinois: Stipes, 1978.

IV.

OUTCOMES

We now have an understanding of the concept of protocol packages and the elements in their design. Before considering the development of such a package, let us briefly discuss its instructional outcomes. We do this in this chapter by identifying the salient outcomes and limitations of protocol packages and by comparing them with those of other instructional design formats.

Protocol packages deal with interpersonal interactions. The ultimate goal of any worthwhile training in this area is for a person to perform effectively, efficiently, intelligently, and positively in an interpersonal situation. The logic of protocols suggests the sequence in Figure 17 for systematic training in this area.

This scheme suggests that the first step toward our goal of appropriate interpersonal performance is the mastery of a set of concepts. We use these concepts to understand what is happening in an interpersonal situation. This in turn helps us to analyze the situation in terms of different factors influencing it, including our own current behavior. Based on this analysis, we can hypothesize the most appropriate next step. Finally, we are ready to take this step. With our basic conceptual framework, we can monitor the consequences of this behavior, keep continuous track of what is happening in the situation, make informed decisions, and carry them out.

Figure 17

*A Suggested Training Sequence
for Interpersonal Performances*

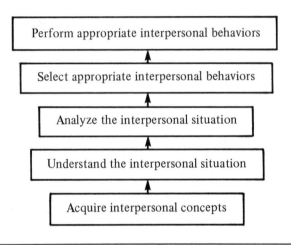

Action resulting from this type of analysis is superior to intuitive action or panic reaction. For a teacher who confronts a screaming child, the automatic response is to shut him or her up. For a parent who catches a child telling a lie, the immediate response is to scold him or her. For a probation officer who meets a hostile juvenile offender, the natural inclination is to threaten him or her. For a husband who finds his wife in tears, the conventional response is to console her. For a store detective who notices someone slipping a radio into her handbag, the instinctive response is to arrest her on the spot. For a principal who faces a group of angry students marching toward his or her office, the protective response is to call the police. In each of these cases, what is automatic, immediate, natural, conventional, instinctive, and protective may not always be the most appropriate action to take.

There is nothing wrong with a quick reaction as long as it is also an appropriate one. In many interpersonal situations, rapid reaction prevents unnecessary damage to individuals or to the group.

There is something wrong with rapid, unthinking action. Action without analysis is undesirable. So is analysis without action. Taking one's own time before acting does not guarantee the appropriateness of the action. Incompetence and fear may contribute to a long delay, and this is not to be confused with deliberate action based on an objective analysis of the situation.

One of the major outcomes.of a protocol package is the facilitation of effective, efficient, and objective analysis of an interpersonal situation. Protocol packages achieve this outcome by providing information and instruction related to all but the top step in Figure 17. Thus, protocol packages have a major weakness: they do not equip the trainee to perform the appropriate interpersonal behavior. The trainee can select the behavior, identify its critical attributes, and recognize it when performed by others. All of this provides a strong base for acquiring the appropriate interpersonal skill, but it is not the same as skill training. This is a major limitation of protocol packages. Unless followed up by appropriate skill training, its outcome is sterile analysis. If our goal is to educate philosophers, a protocol package is sufficient. But if it is to train practitioners, we need to move on to related skill training.

Protocols Versus Training Materials

Many instructional designers feel that protocols emphasize irrelevant theory and are, therefore, inefficient. They would like to go about interpersonal training in the same manner as in developing an army training film on how to strip and assemble an M-16 rifle. As a result, many training films present and produce interpersonal performances by numbers without taking the trouble to build upon a solid conceptual base. They are undoubtedly much more efficient than training that begins with a protocol package—if a specific performance is concerned. However, a protocol base has the following advantageous outcomes compared to these types of training material:

1. Training without theory tells the trainee what to do but not why he or she is to do it. A rationale for our behavior enhances motivation in most instances. Such a rationale is especially important in the area of interpersonal skills, where many of the recommendations apparently go against our intuition and logic.

2. Individual differences play an important role in the acquisition and application of any skill. Different folks need different strokes to accomplish the same outcome. Forcing everyone to perform in the same way is inefficient and inappropriate, especially with interpersonal behaviors. The aptitudes of an individual may not permit him or her to follow a standard procedure in rigid fashion. Not everyone can interact with the humor and charm of someone else. In training material, the focus is on a specific way to behave. In a protocol package, it is on a class of behaviors whose critical attributes are specified. The individual is permitted stylistic variations in his or her performance.

3. Training materials focus on a specific skill and on a specific way to use it. They are of limited transfer value. Protocol packages, in contrast, illustrate a wide range of interpersonal behaviors. This permits the trainee to transfer the skill to an equally wide range of real-life situations.

Protocol Packages Versus Field-Based Training

Many instructional designers agree with the basic premise for protocol packages, but prefer to provide real-life examples of interactive concepts from real life itself. For example, there is an enthusiastic move toward field-based teacher education with the justification that the best way to learn to teach is by doing it and the best place to do it is where teaching usually takes place—in the school. This is an effective strategy if used in conjunction with protocol packages. However, it is not a replacement for the outcomes of a protocol package for three reasons:

1. During the teaching process, the teacher has his or her mind so fully occupied with what has to be done that there is no time for an objective analysis of the interpersonal situation. Throwing a non-swimmer into the water may result in a high level of motivation, but it is also a cruel strategy. Such learning by trauma on the job may work for survival skills but not for systematic analysis.

2. If the trainee merely observes the interpersonal scene without participating in the action, he or she may have more opportunities for calm analysis. However, in the words of Smith and his colleagues (1969), this is not an effective way to acquire the analytical skills because

> behavior perishes as it happens and nothing is left to analyze except the memory or a check sheet. The fidelity of the memory is questionable and not detailed enough. The information contained on check sheets is almost no record at all. To learn to interpret situations, they must be held in situ or reproduced at will approximately as they occurred. (p. 54)

Protocol packages meet the requirement of reproducing the situation at will.

3. Observation of real-life situations lacks the control required for instructional effectiveness. There is no guarantee that the critical types of interpersonal interaction will take place with sufficient clarity and frequency to help the trainee acquire the analytical framework. In contrast, in a protocol package we can ensure an effective scope and sequence of these interpersonal interactions through production and editing techniques.

Protocol Packages Versus Other Instructional Designs

Both protocol and experiential learning packages depend upon learning from experience. Protocol packages use vicarious experiences in a recorded form, and because of this they do not involve the trainee as intensely in the situation as does an experiential learning package (Thiagarajan, 1980). However, a protocol package provides a more controlled and less risky situation.

Similarly, protocol packages do not provide the same degree of active participation as do simulation games (Thiagarajan and Stolovitch, 1978), role playing (Wohlking and Gill, 1980), or Rolemaps (Dormant, 1980). There is no opportunity for the trainee to manipulate the interpersonal environment and to experience the consequences.

Summary

Here are the salient outcomes of a protocol package:

1. A glimpse of reality in an interpersonal situation.

2. Efficient and effective instruction for acquiring a conceptual framework.

3. A conceptual base which provides a rationale for recommended interpersonal behaviors.

4. Highly generalizable concepts which identify the critical attributes and the permissible variations for specific classes of interpersonal behaviors.

And here are some important limitations of a protocol package:

1. No active participation in a real or simulated interpersonal experience.

2. No specific training in interpersonal skills.

The outcomes of the protocol packages suggest that they have an important place in the instructional designer's tool kit. The limitations suggest that we should always use them in conjunction with other instructional design formats to create a comprehensive package for integrating theory and practice in the interpersonal area.

References

Dormant, D. *Rolemaps.* Englewood Cliffs, New Jersey: Educational Technology Publications, 1980.

Smith, B.O. *et al. Teachers for the Real World.* Washington, D.C.: American Association of Colleges for Teacher Education, 1969.

Thiagarajan, S. *Experiential Learning Packages.* Englewood Cliffs, New Jersey: Educational Technology Publications, 1980.

Thiagarajan, S., and Stolovitch, H.D. *Instructional Simulation Games.* Englewood Cliffs, New Jersey: Educational Technology Publications, 1978.

Wohlking, W., and Gill, P. *Role Playing.* Englewood Cliffs, New Jersey: Educational Technology Publications, 1980.

V.

DEVELOPMENTAL GUIDE

This chapter deals with the production of protocol packages. It assumes that you are familiar with the concepts from the previous chapters. It presents a set of initial guidelines for the development of your protocol package. These guidelines are incomplete; actual experience and additional reading are needed to supplement them.

The developmental process presented in this chapter is an adaptation of the usual "systems" model for instructional development. The five major stages in this model are analysis, design, production, evaluation/revision, and implementation.

The purpose of the *analysis* stage is to specify the need for a protocol package, to identify the relevant characteristics of trainees, and to define the conceptual domain.

The purpose of the *design* stage is to come up with a detailed blueprint for the protocol package. This blueprint specifies the types and functions of different media, strategies for production and editing, and the scope and sequence of the content.

The purpose of the *production* stage is to create a prototype package. This involves the recording of the protocol component and the creation of the instructional component.

The purpose of the *evaluation/revision* stage is to improve the effectiveness of the protocol package. This involves making modifications to the package on the basis of the feedback from experts and trainees.

The purpose of the *implementation* stage is to prepare a final version of the protocol package, to make potential users aware of its existence, and to facilitate adoption.

This chapter does *not* include guidelines for the stages of physical production and implementation. This is not because these two stages are not important—actually we would argue that they are the two most important stages—but because the amount of technical detail is beyond the scope of this book.

Analysis

The analysis stage is an attempt to provide answers to the following questions:

1. Do you really need a protocol package?
2. Who will use your protocol?
3. In what situation will your protocol package be used?
4. What is your basic approach to protocol development?
5. What is the purpose of your protocol package?
6. What concepts are you going to teach?

Let us explore procedures for finding answers to each of these questions.

Do You Really Need a Protocol Package?

The production of an effective protocol package requires considerable investments of time and other resources. Protocol packages frequently suffer from an apparent lack of relevance, which becomes real if they are produced arbitrarily. Because of these two reasons, it is very important to undertake an objective needs analysis and ensure that the protocol package would be cost-effective. In general, you can be sure of the need for a protocol package, if you can answer "yes" to the following questions:

- *Is the trainee prevented from effective performance due to a lack of knowledge?*

- *Does the trainee's performance require analyzing and interpreting situations that involve interpersonal interaction?*
- *Is a conceptual framework available for the analysis of these situations?*
- *Can you record these realistic examples in a cost-effective fashion?*

Who Will Use Your Protocol?

The answer to this question is obtained through learner analysis which uses these component questions:

- *What background experience do trainees already have?*
- *What major misconceptions and stereotypes are the trainees likely to have?*
- *What is the attitude of the trainees toward the content of your protocol package?*
- *What media preferences and processing skills do the trainees have?*

In What Situation Will Your Protocol Package Be Used?

Here are some sample questions for this type of context analysis:

- *Who are the trainers? What are their experiences, competencies, and preferences?*
- *How does the protocol package fit within the overall training program?*
- *What media facilities are available in the training situation? What are the scheduling constraints? How long can your protocol package last?*

> • *What are the budget constraints? How much can your institution afford for the development of your protocol package?*

What Is Your Basic Approach to Protocol Development?

The design of a protocol package can begin with either of these two bases:

- a conceptual framework, or
- a complex interactive situation.

Many of the procedures recommended in this chapter are applicable to both approaches to protocol development. However, the order in which the procedures are undertaken differs. In the "concept-first" approach (Thiagarajan, Semmel, and Semmel, 1974), we begin with a concept analysis and organize the protocol component to reflect this analysis. In the "situation-first" approach (Cruickshank, 1974), we begin with a representative protocol situation and apply the concept analysis procedure to it. In this approach, the protocol component organizes the instructional component, while in the previous approach, it is the other way around.

The guidelines that follow support the "concept-first" approach. Supplementary suggestions for the "situation-first" approach are given later.

The selection of which approach to take is a simple decision. Ask yourself the question, "Do I want to teach a prespecified conceptual framework?" If the answer is "Yes," you should use the "concept-first" approach. If the answer is "No," you are more likely to benefit from the "situation-first" approach.

What Is the Purpose of Your Protocol Package?

All protocol packages deal with the acquisition of conceptual frameworks. However, the exact purposes of different protocol packages may be different. In this stage of analysis, you determine the primary purpose of your protocol package. The following checklist summarizes the discussion from the first chapter and serves as a handy reminder of appropriate uses for a protocol package:

I. BACKGROUND INSTRUCTION

1. Increasing the levels of awareness of trainees **in an area of human interaction which is to be studied in greater detail.**

2. Providing advance organizers **to a conceptual framework so that trainees can organize more specific information within this framework.**

3. Modeling of skills **which incorporate different concepts related to interpersonal interactions.**

4. Stimulating a group discussion **to facilitate sharing of existing conceptual frameworks.**

II. DIRECT INSTRUCTION

5. Teaching concepts **related to interactive behaviors.**

6. Training observers **on the use of behavioral checklists and observation systems.**

III. EVALUATION OF INSTRUCTION

7. Evaluation of concept mastery.

8. Evaluation of coder reliability.

9. Formative evaluation of instruction.

10. Summative evaluation of instruction.

IV. ANALYSIS OF INSTRUCTION

11. Learner and context analyses **in initial stages of instructional development.**

12. Task and concept analyses **to specify the objectives and content for an instructional package.**

What Concepts Are You Going to Teach?

Concept analysis is a systematic procedure for exploring individual concepts, their definitions, their characteristics, and their interrelationships. Many excellent instructional materials (Engelmann, 1969; Merrill and Tennyson, 1977; Wilson, 1963) provide guidance in this area. I have found the work of Susan Markle and Philip Tiemann (Markle and Tiemann, 1970; Tiemann and Markle, 1978) particularly elegant and effective; the following guidelines are primarily based on this source.

Here are the major steps in a concept analysis for a protocol package:

1. Identify a specific domain of human interactions and list relevant concepts in this domain.

2. Arrange the concepts in a hierarchy and identify missing, redundant, and superfluous items.

3. Select a concept from the lowest level of your hierarchy and write a working definition.

4. Identify the critical and variable attributes of this concept.

5. Generate sets of examples and nonexamples for use in teaching and testing this concept.

6. Repeat this procedure with other coordinate concepts.

7. Identify the necessary attributes among different concepts at different levels of the hierarchy.

Here are brief explanations and examples of these steps:

1. The domain of human interaction. In this initial step, you specify the general area for your protocol package and identify a list of relevant concepts within that area. A productive thinking approach (such as brainstorming) is more useful than any deductive approach during this step.

---

*Let's assume that we are interested in **discipline problems** as the domain of human interaction. As a* *result of our brainstorming, we come up with this random list of concepts relevant to this domain: punishment, vandalism, disruptive behavior, juvenile delinquents, rights of students, dress code, withdrawal, disobedience, name-calling, threatening the teacher, physical assault, refusal to cooperate, loyalty, obedient children, talking out of turn, behavior modification, bullying, communication, reinforcement, contingency management, empathy, life-space interviews, authority, value clarification, sarcasm, criticism, teachers' rights, fear, parental cooperation, report cards, . . .*

2. The concept hierarchy. The results of brainstorming are at different levels of specificity: Some concepts are narrow, while others are broad. In contrast to the open-ended activity of the previous step, we use a tight, logical activity in this step. We classify the concepts into appropriate categories and organize them into a hierarchy. In this process, we may come across superfluous concepts which do not fit into the hierarchy. We may also come across redundant labels for the same concept. The symmetry of our hierarchy may suggest gaps in our framework.

Hierarchies are artificial creations of the analyst; they do not exist in the real world. The concepts and their interrelationships reflect the current literature. But when there are no pre-established conventions, the analyst can make arbitrary decisions to increase the efficiency and the effectiveness of acquiring the concepts and applying them.

The final results of organizing our brainstormed concepts into a hierarchy are shown as Figure 2 in Chapter I. In the process of setting up and refining this hierarchy, some concepts (e.g., vandalism, students' rights) which dealt with legal aspects were dropped from the domain. Narrow concepts were combined into broader ones. For example, threatening the teacher, name-calling, and bullying were all subsumed under the concept of **verbal agression.** *The parallel nature of verbal and physical interactions helps us to identify some missing items so that the final hierarchy contains these concepts:*

- *Verbal interaction, verbal resistance, verbal aggression, and*
- *physical interaction, physical resistance, physical aggression.*

3. Definition of a single concept. We are now ready to initiate the analysis of a single concept. We begin by giving the concept a convenient name and by writing down a tentative definition. At this stage, getting something down on paper is much more important than rigorous logic. The definition usually describes the superordinate concept and gives the critical attributes of the behaviors which belong to this class. It is very unlikely that this definition will remain unchanged at the end of the analysis.

We select the concept of **verbal aggression** *for our first analysis. This is an arbitrary decision probably based on some incident we observed in a classroom that day. This is our working definition:*

Verbal aggression is an act of student defiance which is directed against the teacher.

4. Critical and variable attributes of the concept. We are now ready to refine our concept by identifying its critical and variable attributes.

• Begin by thinking up an obvious example. Make a list of its salient attributes.

An obvious example of verbal aggression involves a tough-looking inner-city teenager screaming obscenities at the teacher. This interaction contains the following characteristics:

- *The student is screaming at the **teacher**.*
- *He or she appears to be **angry**.*
- *The teacher is **frightened**.*
- *The teacher has done nothing to **provoke** this insult.*
- *The content of the student's statement is **obscene**.*
- *The student is **moving** toward the teacher.*

• Vary the situation in the example by changing one attribute at a time. If it is no longer an example (i.e., if it becomes a *nonexample*), then that attribute is a critical one. Otherwise, it is a variable attribute.

---

*We take the first attribute in your imaginary interaction: **first characteristic**: The student is screaming at the **teacher**. If we substitute a **student** for the teacher, do we still have an example of verbal aggression? We decide that we do, and therefore we decide that the person being screamed at is a variable attribute. Using the same process, we check out the next attribute: He or she appears to be **angry**. Keeping the other things the same, do we still have an example if the student appears to be **friendly**? We decide that it is more likely to be a friendly interaction. Therefore, **anger** is a critical attribute.*

> *We also notice the incongruity of a person who is friendly, while his or her statements are abusive. As Tiemann and Markle (1978) point out, this is a signal that we have redundant critical attributes. Either the angry appearance or the content of the abusive statement is a sufficient indicator of the underlying critical attribute:* **The person is hostile.**

- *Conjure up more examples and nonexamples.* Do not stay with the same example for too long. Make your new examples different from the previous ones. Gradually move toward the borderline area where the examples are so subtle (and the nonexamples are so close-in) that you have a problem deciding whether it is an example or not. Take an attribute of the concept and push it to its limits. You may be forced to make some arbitrary decisions about your definition.

> *We came up with these subtle examples of* **verbal aggression***:*
> *A student is whispering softly to another in the next seat. You really have to listen carefully to realize the sarcastic and hostile intent of the message.*
> *Another student is directing very strong words against the teacher, but he or she is reading a passage from a dramatic anthology at the request of the teacher.*
> *Pushing the amount of hostility to the extreme, we came up with the incident of a student talking very little but systematically clobbering another student.*

5. Specification of examples and nonexamples. In concept analysis, we refine our tentative definition by examining examples and nonexamples. Our collection of critical and variable attributes becomes a revised definition of the concept. We now work backwards and generate sets of examples and nonexamples of the concept:

• List the critical attributes and create nonexamples by leaving out one attribute at a time.

This is the list of critical attributes we identified for **verbal aggression***:*

1. It is an interaction initiated by a student.

2. It is hostile.

3. It is directed toward another person.

4. It does not involve physical violence.

Here are examples of the nonexample obtained by leaving out one critical attribute at a time:

1. A teacher is angrily shouting at a student.

2. One student is talking angrily to another, but as part of a rehearsal for a play.

3. A student is extremely angry about a stupid mistake he or she made, and he or she berates himself or herself in a loud voice.

4. A student is screaming and punching everyone around him or her.

• List the variable attributes and create a pool of divergent examples.

We finally decide that these are the variable attributes of **verbal aggression***:*

1. Content of the verbal message.

2. Target of aggression.

3. Reason for the aggressive act.

> *4. Intensity of aggression.*
> *The pool of divergent examples contains clean and dirty messages directed toward the teacher, students, and other school personnel. Some of the acts are spontaneous, while others were provoked. Some are loud, uncontrolled, and accompanied by gestures and threatening motions, while others are cool, controlled, and delivered with a dead-pan expression.*

6. Continuing individual concept analyses. The previous procedure is now repeated with other concepts at the same level of the hierarchy. As more and more of these individual analyses are undertaken, the process becomes simpler because of the coordinate nature of the concepts. The types of question used with one concept suggest similar questions for another; the nonexamples of one concept suggest examples for another.

> *We carry out the same procedure with verbal interaction, verbal resistance, physical interaction, physical resistance, physical aggression, withdrawal, noise, and so on from the concept hierarchy. (As you may notice, the sequence is not entirely arbitrary.)*

7. Hierarchies and necessary attributes. In analyzing coordinate concepts, we identify some critical attributes shared by all individual concepts. These critical attributes are called necessary attributes by Merrill and Tennyson (1977); they define membership in a superordinate concept.

> *One obvious critical attribute shared by the concepts*

> *of physical resistance and physical aggression is* **physical activity.** *This critical attribute is a necessary attribute of the superordinate concept of physical interaction. Similarly,* **verbal activity** *is a necessary attribute of verbal interaction, which includes verbal resistance and verbal aggression. These two superordinate concepts share the necessary attribute of* **student interaction** *at the next higher level of the hierarchy.*

At the completion of the concept analysis, we end up with a hierarchy of concepts which provide the content for the protocol package.

Design

The design stage of our systematic development model begins from where the analysis stage leaves off. During this stage, we specify the variable attributes for our protocol package. We do this by answering the following questions:

- What is the specific objective for our package? At what level of awareness or analysis do we want the trainers to acquire our conceptual framework?
- How do we integrate the instructional and protocol components?
- What medium or media combinations do we want the protocol package to use?
- How much continuity do we provide for the protocol? Is it going to be a single case study, two or three vignettes, or a series of fast-paced 30-second clips?
- What production technique are we going to use: scripted play, open-ended role play, or naturalistic recording?
- How much editing do we need to undertake: minimal

editing to remove minor errors or maximum editing to reduce hours of taping to a short segment?

Most of these alternatives have been discussed in the second chapter of this book. Here are some additional guidelines for the media-selection decision:

1. Identify media attributes that are required to present your protocol and instructional content. These media attributes include sound and visual capabilities, motion, and color.

2. Identify the media attributes required for matching your *learner characteristics* and needs. These attributes include response mode, feedback mode, self-pacing, and random access.

3. Identify the media attributes required for use in your *training context.* These attributes include ease of use, flexibility, compatibility with widely available equipment, and cost.

4. Identify the media attributes required for the effective and efficient *production* of the package. These attributes include local expertise, production cost, editability, and transportability of the equipment to location.

5. List the media equipment available to you. Taking one medium at a time from your list, decide whether each of the media attributes required is available. Compare and contrast the availability of these requirements from different media. Select the medium (or media combination) which provides all of your requirements.

Evaluation and Revision

Usually, evaluation is supposed to begin after the production of an instructional material. We prefer to treat it as a continuing process which begins with the analysis stage and proceeds throughout all stages of development of the protocol package.

The main objective of evaluation is to assess the worth of

the protocol package so that it can be improved. For practical suggestions in this area, we refer you to general books (e.g., Gropper, 1975, and Lawson, 1974) and to the specific case study by Gliessman and Pugh (1976). Here are some initial guidelines which we have found helpful.

Expert Verification and Revision

One type of evaluation for the improvement of the protocol package is expert appraisal of our plans and products. Here are the different materials that can be subjected to this type of evaluation:

- definitions of various concepts,
- hierarchy charts showing the relationships among the concepts,
- descriptions (or scripts) of examples and nonexamples to be presented in the protocol package,
- description of the instructional strategy,
- script for the protocol package,
- instructional materials, and
- prototype version of the protocol package.

Figure 18 is a list of different types of experts and the evaluative feedback they can provide.

Learner Verification and Revision

Although experts can appraise and improve the protocol package in different ways, the real test of its effectiveness comes from actual tryouts with trainees. Here are some guidelines for collecting useful feedback and correcting the weaknesses of the protocol package:

• You do not have to wait for the complete package before you begin your tryouts of the protocol materials. You can test your concepts and examples in a written or script form and obtain useful feedback.

• When you try out the prototype package, make sure that the trainee understands that it is the *material* which is being evaluated. Encourage the trainee to offer critical comments and suggestions for improvement.

• Conduct initial tryout sessions with individual trainees. Proceed to testing in small groups. Eventually, try out the package under field conditions with a typical trainer using the material.

• The purpose of learner verification and revision is not to collect information, but to use it for the improvement of the protocol package. Make suitable changes in the package after one tryout and at the beginning of the next.

Adaptations of the Development Model

The systematic development model presented above is best suited to the "concept-first" approach to the development of a protocol package designed to help the trainees acquire a conceptual framework. In the last section of this chapter, we briefly discuss modifications necessary to make this model more suitable for approaches and purposes.

"Situation-First" Approach to Protocol Development

In the original rationale for protocol materials in teacher training (Smith *et al.,* 1969) and in the practical suggestions by Cruickshank (1974), there is an emphasis on protocols that represent authentic situations. This "situation-first" approach prevents developers from packaging some irrelevant conceptual scheme merely because it has been traditionally taught to trainees. This approach incorporates an adequate needs analysis in the development process. Figure 19 graphically depicts the major differences between the "concept-first" approach (presented earlier) and this "situation-first" approach. Here are some suggestions for adapting our development model to accommodate the needs of the "situation-first" approach:

• Begin by collecting information on authentic interactive situations in the domain selected for the protocol. For

Figure 18

Types of Feedback from Different Experts

Expert	Type of Feedback
Subject-matter expert	Appropriateness of the selected domain of human interaction
	Compatibility between external goals and training objectives
	Adequacy of the definition of concepts
	Accuracy of terms and concept labels
	Authenticity of the examples and non-examples
	Acceptability of the theoretical framework
Instructional designer	Adequacy of concept analysis
	Appropriateness of instructional objectives
	Suitability of the examples and nonexamples
	Effectiveness of the instructional sequence and strategy

(Continued on Next Page)

Figure 18 (Continued)

Experienced trainer	Appropriateness of the protocol package to the needs of the trainees
	Suitability of the package to the training situation
	Flexibility of use by the trainers
	Appropriateness of the level of language and the types of examples
Media production specialist	Suitability of the selected media
	Technical quality of media production
	Aesthetic quality of media production
	Compatibility of the package to generally available media equipment

Figure 19

Differences Between "Concept-First"
and "Situation-First" Approaches to Protocol Development

"Concept-First" Approach: **"Situation-First" Approach:**

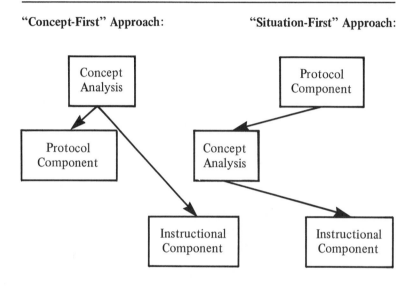

example, if the domain is policy-council meetings, collect information on what happens during these meetings. This can be done through participation in a policy-council meeting, observation, analysis of natural protocol records, and interviews of policy makers with the use of the critical-incident technique.

• Develop a script for representative protocol records. Or, select segments of natural protocols which you feel are authentic representations of policy-council meetings.

• Verify the authenticity of the scripted incidents or sample segments by having a group of policy-council members and experts rate them. Select the most credible records or scripts and develop them into prototype protocol materials. Try these out with practitioners and revise to make them more realistic.

- Analyze the content of your realistic protocols. Identify the conceptual hierarchy, superordinate concepts, individual concepts, and critical attributes by working through these protocols.
- Design the instructional component to present the conceptual framework that helps the trainees to analyze and interpret the protocol component. Integrate this component into a package.

Different Approaches for Different Purposes

Here are a few suggestions for modifying the development model to better match the needs of protocol packages with different purposes:

- *Protocols to increase the levels of awareness.* The emphasis in this type of package is on the authenticity of examples rather than on the instructional component. The "situation-first" approach is recommended when you are developing a protocol package to increase the familiarity of trainees to an interpersonal situation. The ideal production technique is recording natural protocol segments on location and editing them into a coherent collection.
- *Protocols to provide advance organizers.* This type of protocol presents a summary of the entire conceptual hierarchy before the trainees study individual concepts in detail. The development should be based on a comprehensive concept analysis. A fast-paced and tightly edited series of short vignettes is the most appropriate format to serve this purpose.
- *Protocols to stimulate group discussions.* This type of protocol package is best developed through the "situation-first" approach. The incidents in the protocol should be capable of attracting and maintaining the attention of the group of viewers (or listeners). This can be achieved through the selection of critical incidents in the interactive situation. This protocol should also encourage immediate discussion of

the interaction. This can be achieved by terminating the incident in an open-ended fashion without resolving the critical problem. The protocol should elicit existing concepts from members of the groups. This can be achieved by avoiding any heavy-handed instruction.

• *Protocols for training users of an observation system.* Concept analysis for this type of protocol should be based on the behavioral categories of the observation system. As I have suggested elsewhere (Thiagarajan, 1973), the development of the observation system and the protocol package should go hand-in-hand in order to obtain relevant training and reliable coding.

• *Protocols for evaluation.* The validity of protocol materials for evaluation can be increased by recording naturalistic events and editing the tapes to represent samples of all relevant categories of behavior. Its objectivity can be increased through the careful preparation of a scoring key. This can be done by having a panel of experts carefully analyze the protocol incidents, stopping and replaying the tape to clarify any doubts.

Summary

Systematic development of a protocol package involves the stages of analysis, design, production, evaluation/revision, and implementation. The key to an effective and efficient protocol package is a concept analysis. In the case of the "concept-first" approach, this analysis precedes the production of the protocol record; in the case of the "situation-first" approach, the sequence is reversed. Specific media, production techniques, and the amount of editing should be determined according to the intents and the contents of the protocol package.

References

Cruickshank, D.R. The Protocol Materials Movement: One Exemplar of Efforts to Wed Theory and Practice in Teacher Education. *Journal of Teacher Education,* 1974, *25*(4).

Engelmann, S. *Conceptual Learning.* San Rafael, California: Dimensions Publishing Company, 1969.

Gliessman, D., and Pugh, R.C. The Development and Evaluation of Protocol Films of Teacher Behavior. *AV Communication Review,* 1976, *24*(1).

Gropper, G.L. *Diagnosis and Revision in the Development of Instructional Materials.* Englewood Cliffs, New Jersey: Educational Technology Publications, 1975.

Lawson, T.E. *Formative Instructional Product Evaluation.* Englewood Cliffs, New Jersey: Educational Technology Publications, 1974.

Markle, S.M., and Tiemann, P.W. *Really Understanding Concepts, or in Frumious Pursuit of the Jabberwock.* Champaign, Illinois: Stipes, 1970.

Merrill, M.D., and Tennyson, R.D. *Teaching Concepts: An Instructional Design Guide.* Englewood Cliffs, New Jersey: Educational Technology Publications, 1977.

Smith, B.O. *et al.* Teachers for the Real World. Washington, D.C.: American Association of Colleges for Teacher Education, 1969.

Thiagarajan, S. Instructional Systems for Interactional Systems. *Classroom Interaction Newsletter,* 1973, *9*(1).

Thiagarajan, S., Semmel, D.S., and Semmel, M.I. *Instructional Development for Training Teachers of Exceptional Children: A Sourcebook.* Reston, Virginia: The Council for Exceptional Children, 1974.

Tiemann, P.W., and Markle, S.M. *Analyzing Instructional Content: A Guide to Instruction and Evaluation.* Champaign, Illinois: Stipes, 1978.

Wilson, J. *Thinking with Concepts.* Cambridge, England: Cambridge University Press, 1963.

VI.

RESOURCES

Clark, D.C. Teaching Concepts in the Classroom: A Set of Teaching Prescriptions Derived from Experimental Research. *Journal of Educational Psychology,* 1971, *62*(3), 253-278.

Cruickshank, D.R. The Protocol Materials Movement: One Exemplar of Efforts to Wed Theory and Practice in Teacher Education. *Journal of Teacher Education,* 1974, *25*(4).

Engelmann, S. *Conceptual Learning.* San Rafael, California: Dimensions Publishing Company, 1969.

Glaser, R. Concept Learning and Concept Teaching. In R.M. Gagne and W.J. Gephart (Eds.), *Learning Research and School Subjects.* Itasca, Illinois: F.E. Peacock Publishers, 1969.

Gliessman, D., and Pugh, R.C. The Development and Evaluation of Protocol Films of Teacher Behavior. *AV Communication Review,* 1976, *24*(1).

Hudgins, B.B. The Portrayal of Concepts: An Issue in the Development of Protocol Materials. In *Acquiring Teaching Competencies: Reports and Studies.* Bloomington, Indiana: Center for the Development of Training Materials in Teacher Education, 1971.

Jackson, D.A., Della-Piana, G.M., and Sloane, H.N. *How to Establish a Behavior Observation System.* Englewood

Cliffs, New Jersey: Educational Technology Publications, 1975.

Markle, S.M., and Tiemann, P.W. *Really Understanding Concepts, or in Frumious Pursuit of the Jabberwock.* Champaign, Illinois: Stipes, 1970.

Markle, S.M., and Tiemann, P.W. Conceptual Learning and Instructional Design. *Educational Technology,* 1970, *1*(1).

Martorella, P.H. *Concept Learning: Designs for Instruction.* Scranton, Pennsylvania: Intext Educational Publishers, 1972.

Merrill, M.D., and Tennyson, R.D. *Teaching Concepts: An Instructional Design Guide.* Englewood Cliffs, New Jersey: Educational Technology Publications, 1977.

Simon, A., and Boyer, E.G. (Eds.) *Mirrors for Behavior: An Anthology of Observation Instruments.* Philadelphia: Research for Better Schools, 1970.

Smith, B.O. *et al. Teachers for the Real World.* Washington, D.C.: American Association of Colleges for Teacher Education, 1969.

Thiagarajan, S. Instructional Systems for Interactional Systems. *Classroom Interaction Newsletter,* 1973, *9*(1).

Thiagarajan, S. Making Protocol Films: An Exercise in Concept Teaching. *Educational Technology,* 1975, *2*(3).

Thiagarajan, S., and Semmel, M.I. Observation Systems and the Special Education Teacher. *Focus on Exceptional Children,* 1973, *5*(7).

Thiagarajan, S., Semmel, D.S., and Semmel, M.I. *Instructional Development for Training Teachers of Exceptional Children: A Sourcebook.* Reston, Virginia: The Council for Exceptional Children, 1974.

Tiemann, P.W., and Markle, S.M. *Analyzing Instructional Content: A Guide to Instruction and Evaluation.* Champaign, Illinois: Stipes, 1978.

SIVASAILAM ("THIAGI") THIAGARAJAN is a free-lance trainer, instructional developer, and performance technologist. He is currently working in Gbarnga, Liberia, providing technical assistance to the Ministry of Education on improving the efficiency of elementary school instruction through the application of programmed teaching and learning technologies. Thiagi began his career in education in Madras, India, where he taught high school physics and math for six years. His home-grown instructional innovations attracted the attention of Dr. Douglas Ellson, who invited him to work on a project at Indiana University. Thiagi received his Ph.D in Instructional Systems Technology from Indiana University. His professional experiences in the United States include administering six major instructional development projects, consulting with 40 organizations, and conducting more than 100 workshops all over the country. Thiagi has been the president of the National Society for Performance and Instruction (NSPI) and the Association for Special Education Technology (ASET). He is a prolific writer and has published 12 books, more than 100 articles, 30 audio-visual training packages, and 15 simulations/games. He has been the editor of three professional journals and served on the editorial board of four others.